Why Do Men
Believe Evolution
Against All Odds?

Also by Dr. Carl Baugh

*Dinosaur: Scientific Evidence that Man
and Dinosaurs Walked Together*

Panorama of Creation

Creation in Symphony: The Evidence

Creation in Symphony: The Model

Printed in China

ISBN 1-933641-02-9

Why Do Men
Believe Evolution
Against All Odds?

Carl Baugh, Ph.D.

illustrations by Steve Miller

Table of Contents

Foreword

"In every major issue, the majority is always wrong." Many years ago, a dear friend and fellow-believer posited that statement in many of his lectures. I was reminded of his thesis as I read the latest book of another dear friend, Dr. Carl Baugh, entitled *Why Do Men Believe Evolution Against All Odds?* As I have assessed the two sides of the creation/evolution controversy from a practical engineering point of view, I have re-echoed the question posed in the book's title—How can anyone believe that the unbounded complexity of living things can arise from inanimate matter without the Hand and Mind of our Almighty Creator?

It has been especially difficult to contemplate how such belief can be generated as I have studied the intricacies of the human cardiovascular system in my own biomechanics research. The needs of our bodies are so wonderfully met with such adroit designs that one can only stand in awe of the end result. As we come to know more and more of our own makeup, as scientists probe deeper and deeper into the basic building blocks of our bodies, it becomes increasingly difficult to see how evolutionary thinking with its crude and oft-counterproductive developmental tools has any followers. Yet, we know that the majority of the intellectual populace is ardent in its belief in evolution. To use a modern phrase: It boggles the mind! This dilemma is one that Dr. Baugh has set for himself to unravel.

In an impressive display of evidence covering the pertinent categories of the creation/evolution controversy, Dr. Baugh marshals statement after statement from the literature showing the impossibility of the evolutionary mechanisms. He delves into the origin of life issues, the stasis problem, and the record of the fossils. His chapter on design, a prominent topic in the current controversy, covers the spectrum of evidence and proves once again Paley's original statement: "Design requires a Designer!"

In his last chapter, Dr. Baugh gives us some truly insightful analysis of the mindset of the one man most inextricably associated with evolutionary theory—Charles Darwin. Darwin, 1859, held a completely erroneous view of the structure and composition of the basic building block of life forms—his "simple" cell. His view was the scientific view of his day, there being no means by which our present-day information could have been determined. If Michael Behe's book, *Darwin's Black Box,* had carried an 1858 publishing date, how far would Darwin's theory have flown? Although the answer should be, "It would never have gotten off the ground," we know that men do believe in evolution against *all* odds; and so we probably would have the same controversy we are having today.

Although others have written extensively about the life and the mental and moral state of the "founder" of the evolutionary theory, Charles Darwin, this book speculates on new interpretations of these aspects of his thought process as it relates to the theory he developed. Ideas have consequences and Darwin's transformation from belief into rebellion against his Creator evidently resulted in a chaotic mindset that turned him into an invalid.

The thought sequence I found most rewarding occurred in the last several pages of the book where, in answering the "four great questions of life," the evolution answers are succinctly contrasted with the creation answers. It is certainly against all odds that anyone would choose the *questionable identity,* the *uncertain past,* the *meaningless present,* and the *hopeless future* of the former over the *identity of great value,* the *designed origin,* the *meaningful purpose,* and the *unlimited future hope* of the latter. Dr. Baugh set a difficult task for himself when he questioned in his title "Why do men believe in evolution?" It is doubtful that anyone can fully answer that question, but he goes a long way toward that end.

—M. E. Clark, Emeritus Professor, College of
Engineering, University of Illinois

Introduction

Creation is an awesome contemplation. With an inheritance derived from its origin, we are endowed with a preoccupation to ask, "Who am I?" "Where did I come from?" "What is my purpose here?" and "Where am I going?"

As creatures of intuitive reflection, we naturally want to know the answer to *"Who* or *what* started all this?" And, as creatures of destiny, we deserve an answer. In our search for answers to origins and personal meaning, each is responsible for arriving at a logical and defensible position *based in evidence.* Ultimately, *we must find the answer for ourselves;* for, in turn, we must live with the consequences of our conclusions.

As reflective observers, we should be able to ask our questions and embrace our conclusions with intellectual freedom, without personal or academic censorship. In fact, the National Academy of Sciences has issued *An Affirmation of Freedom of Inquiry and Expression.* It states specifically

> that the search for knowledge and understanding of the physical universe and of the living things that inhabit it should be conducted under conditions of intellectual freedom, without religious, political, or ideological restrictions . . . without political censorship and without fear of retribution in consequence of unpopularity of their conclusions. . . . Those who challenge existing theories must be protected from retaliatory reactions.[1]

It is the conviction of this researcher that every human soul who is endowed with normal intelligence arrives at a "moment of truth." This experience inevitably provides an inner *confirmation* or *confrontation* with the landmarks encountered during our personal search. Sooner or later, it is "embrace" or "reject," and the consequences are enormous. An inner world-view (and life-philosophy) is ultimately adopted and followed in practice. For some individuals, this practice is in public display; for some, in private preferences; for some, in subtle influences. For each it is a very personal encounter, and the tranquility (or turmoil) can last a lifetime.

Ultimately and personally, we are compelled to come to grips with this question of "life origins." And, it is the considered opinion of veteran scholars that we either arrived by a naturalistic process called *evolution* or a designed procedure called *creation*. There is no third alternative. Scholastic evolutionist D. J. Futuyama sums it up:

> Creation and evolution, between them, exhaust the possible explanations for the origin of living things. Organisms either appeared on the earth fully developed or they did not. If they did not, they must have developed from preexisting species by some process of modification. If they did appear in a fully developed state, they must indeed have been created by some omnipotent intelligence.[2]

1. National Academy of Science, *"Affirmation of Freedom of Inquiry and Expression"*
2. D. J. Futuyama, *Science on Trial*, Pantheon Books, 1983, p.197

Chapter 1

Marks of Evolution

Many sincere, but uninformed, participants in the controversy between creation and evolution hold to the notion that the two concepts can ultimately be harmonized. They fail to realize the enormous gulf between the two positions. William Provine, professor of biological sciences at Cornell University, pointedly wrote:

> As Jacques Monod, E. O. Wilson, and many other biologists have pointed out, modern evolutionary biology has shattered the hope that some kind of designing or purposive force guided human evolution and established the basis of moral rules. Instead, biology leads to a wholly mechanistic view of life. . . . There are no gods and no designing forces. The frequently made assertion that modern biology and assumptions of the Judeo-Christian tradition are fully compatible is false.[1]

Duane Gish of the Creation Research Institute points out that "creation and evolution involve fundamentally different world views,"[2] and then quotes R. Lewontin:

> Yet, whatever our understanding of the social struggle that gives rise to creationism, whatever the desire to reconcile science and religion may be, there is no escape from the fundamental contradiction between evolution and creationism. They are irreconcilable world views.[3]

It is, therefore, important to recognize that (a) **naturalistic evolution cannot be harmonized with special creation.**

■ ■ ■ ■ ■ ■ ■

To the surprise of many casual observers, and to the embarrassment of many journalistic influences, evolution has never been demonstrated to be a viable explanation for life origins (or cosmic origins for that matter). By definition the scientific method requires that the objects or events under study must be **observable, repeatable, and refutable**. Evolution certainly cannot be observed or repeated in the field or in the laboratory. With this in mind, evolutionist Karl Popper, the honored referee of the modern scientific method, pointed out: "It follows that any controversy over the question whether events which are in principle unrepeatable and unique ever do occur cannot be decided by science; it would be a metaphysical controversy."[4]

In his introduction to a 1971 publication of Darwin's *Origin of Species*, L. Harrison Matthews, British biologist and evolutionist, wrote:

> The fact of evolution is the backbone of biology, and biology is thus in the peculiar position of being a science founded on an unproved theory—is it then a science or a faith? Belief in the theory of evolution is thus exactly parallel to belief in special creation—both are concepts which believers know to be true but neither, up to the present, has been capable of proof.[5]

Intense controversy has erupted within the evolutionary camp. *Newsweek* featured an article by Sharon Begley titled "Science Contra Darwin." She revealed:

The great body of work derived from Charles Darwin's revolutionary 1859 book, *On the Origin of Species*, is under increasing attack—and not just from creationists.... So heated is the debate that one Darwinian says there are times when he thinks about going into a field with more intellectual honesty: the used car business.[6]

Evolutionist Michael Denton wrote that the evolutionary paradigm was ". . . an idea which is more like a principle of medieval astrology than a serious twentieth century theory. . . ."[7]

It has been demonstrated throughout the scientific literature that (b) **naturalistic evolution cannot be supported scientifically.**

■ ■ ■ ■ ■ ■ ■

Various naturalistic theories for *life origins* have been suggested from antiquity, and some have been reintroduced with novel variations long before the days of Charles Darwin. Yet, each bold and ingenious explanation is met with scientific research that reduces its plausibility to unfounded speculation. Competent academic researchers such as Sir Frederic Hoyle and Chandra Wickramasinghe have published that

the likelihood that the formation of life from inanimate matter is one to a number with 40,000 noughts after it. . . . It is big enough to bury Darwin and the whole theory of evolution. There was no primeval soup, neither on this planet nor any other, and if the beginnings of life were not random, they must therefore have been the product of purposeful design.[8]

Professor Leslie E. Orgel, one of the world's leading evolutionary biochemists, has written extensively on this difficult subject. He recognizes our fact in point as follows:

> It is extremely improbable that proteins and nucleic acids, both of which are structurally complex, arose spontaneously in the same place at the same time. Yet it also seems impossible to have one without the other. And so, at first glance, one might have to conclude that life could never, in fact, have originated by chemical means.[9]

In spite of the religious fervor with which it is held (c) **naturalistic evolution cannot explain the origin of life.**

■ ■ ■ ■ ■ ■ ■

There is more to the quest than **embracing** answers about our initial beginnings; there is the matter of **being embraced** by the issues of life. Life happens to all of us: we must live with it, and we must die with it! A spontaneous assemblage of interrelated life-hues brushes us each day, and our inner response to the myriad variations depends on our underlying world view. Naturalism offers no companion in victory, and no consolation in despair.

Science News reported that University of Texas at Arlington researcher Raymond Eve administered an extensive survey regarding the underlying convictions held by creationists and evolutionists. He found that a high percentage of professional people were creationists. From the survey data assembled, the researcher admitted that "science can't tell you what the meaning of life is, why we're here, or how to handle bereavement or guilt."[10]

Any interested observer must admit that (d) **naturalistic evolution cannot address the issues of life.**

. . . .

Editor Carl Zimmer of *Discover Magazine* writes about the future demise of Planet Earth. He refers to a "vision of the end."[11] Jeffrey Winters enlarges on the theme to muse about the death of the universe. "How will the universe end? . . . What lies ahead for the universe? Will it expand forever, all its matter thinning into cold, dark wisps? Or will the cosmos eventually collapse into a Big Crunch?"[12]

Those who regard the universe simply as a materialistic expression hold to three alternatives in the fate of the cosmos:

1. The Big Freeze (continued expansion ultimately resulting in heat death)
2. The Big Crunch (eventual collapse of universe upon itself)
3. The Big Fizzle (eventual dissipation of structured energy)

Recently a college chemistry professor asserted that his "ultimate hope was that the elements of his body would provide the chemical nutrients for plants in the next generation." Such an attitude regards this life as all there is —and its inconsistencies as natural chemical disarray. The consequence of holding to a concept void of design, purpose, and hope is that the devotee finds himself *in harmony with an inharmonious cosmos.* He is in harmony with a life in conflict. All the inconsistencies, suffering, and chaos are considered as natural ingredients in a purposeless universe. In a very real sense (e) **naturalistic evolution offers no personal hope.**

■ ■ ■ ■ ■ ■ ■

The *London Times* published an article underlining the never-ending conflict between the two concepts and the ever-widening battle lines engulfing each new generation. The writer, Stuart Wavel, revealed a new scientific challenge to the "old theory" of evolution: that organic molecular systems are **irreducibly complex and require a designer.** He underscored the consequence of adopting evolution as a mindset "that we are self-replicating robots who inhabit a bleak universe without purpose."[13]

These inner pangs and conflicting embracements are actually a vital part of the landscape from the evolutionary point of view. Charles Darwin, the hero of the naturalist's saga, lived with lifelong emotional and mental turmoil. Modern researchers are recognizing that his phobia-laden disposition was corollary to his theories of universal chaos and disarray. He was the first man in history to suggest that his unstable mind was the chaotic universe realizing its own existence. To him the lack of personal peace was as natural as colliding stars. But serious studies of his unnatural obsessions are now being published by scholars on both sides of the aisle. Researchers make reference to "his incessive hypochondria (which some writers maintain was a psychoneurosis related to his anti-religious guilt feelings)."[14]

Irving Stone is an ardent evolutionary humanist and profound admirer of Charles Darwin. He is also the author of a bestselling biography of Darwin. Yet, this biographer candidly noted:

> Darwin returned to England at twenty-seven in a robust state of mind and body. It was not until a year later, when he began to write in his evolutionary notebooks, that he

first felt and commented on his illness, forcing himself into a lifetime of severe, repugnant, and sometimes ludicrous disability.[15]

From the musings of its founder to the contemplation of its most recent convert, naturalistic (f) **evolution can provide no lasting peace.**

■ ■ ■ ■ ■ ■

It should come as no surprise that adamant devotees often insist on publ-ic assertions and unfounded statements, displays that sometimes hide the real reason for their naturalistic commitment. One such unflinching devotee was the great agnostic philosopher Aldous Huxley. Late in his life he offered open discussion on this very issue when he wrote:

Does the world as a whole possess the value and meaning that we constantly attribute to certain parts of it (such as human beings and their works): and, if so, what is the nature of that value and meaning? This is a question which, a few years ago, I should not even have posed. For, like so many of my contemporaries, I took it for granted that there was no meaning. This was partly due to the fact that I shared a common belief that the scientific picture of an abstraction from reality was a true picture of reality as a whole; partly also to other, nonintellectual reasons. I had motives for not wanting the world to have a meaning; consequently assumed that it had none, and was able without any difficulty to find satisfying reasons for this assumption.

Most ignorance is evincible ignorance. We don't know because we don't want to know. It is our will that decides how and upon what subjects we shall use our intelligence. Those who detect no meaning in the world generally do so because, for one reason or another, it suits their books that the world should be meaningless.

. . . For myself as, no doubt, for most of my contemporaries, the philosophy of meaninglessness was essentially an instrument of liberation. The liberation we desired was simultaneously liberation from a certain political and economic system and liberation from a certain system of morality. We objected to the morality because it interfered with our sexual freedom. . .

The supporters of these systems claimed that in some way they embodied meaning (a Christian meaning, they insisted) of the world. There was one admirably simple method of confuting these people and at the same time justifying ourselves in our political and erotic revolt: we could deny that the world had any meaning whatsoever.[16]

Assertions pioneered by these patriarchs of evolution have encouraged succeeding generations to justify their own mindset—all the while ignoring the scientific futility confronting evolutionary explanations. This is done without objective accountability, either to factual research or moral consequences.

Philosopher James Rachels catapults this concept into the modern mindframe. He boldly asserts that

Darwinism undermines both the idea that man is made in the image of God and the idea that man is a unique rational being. Furthermore, if Darwinism is correct, it is unlikely that any other support for the idea of human dignity will be found.[17]

(g) Naturalistic evolution concerns itself with no meaningful dignity or future accountability.

．．．．．．．

In a universe endowed with original design and inherent purpose, current events harmonize with ultimate destiny. The shadings of sorrow and pain enhance the backdrop of peace and joy. Conflict and inconsistencies are unnatural to the original world of order, and will one day be removed from the universal scene.

To the committed evolutionist the approach is entirely different. The agony and purposelessness are part of the natural landscape. The inner conflict and convulsive need to harbor inconsistencies about life and the cosmos underpins a Darwinian mindset. He recorded in his *Autobiography:*

> [Consider] . . . the view now held by most physicists, namely that the sun with all the planets will in time grow too cold for life. . . . Believing as I do that man in the distant future will be a far more perfect creature than he now is, it is an intolerable thought that he and all the other sentient beings are doomed to complete annihilation after such long-continued progress.[18]

Yet he held to that *"intolerable thought"* and actually incubated the agony with relish. (h) **Naturalistic evolution cannot reconcile the present events with future destiny.**

．．．．．．．

The accomplishments of a lifetime are intended to reflect the character, and produce the respect, due an individual who exercised his time and place in the universe. Meaningful accomplishments are often reflected against hardship and overwhelming odds. Dreams are dreamed, plans are planned, and lives are lived with an ever–accumulating memory bank of meaning and purpose.

But written within the fabric of evolutionary thought is an adherence to the inalterable demise of the universe, brought about by cosmic expansion and loss of available energy. The English philosopher Bertrand Russell eloquently expressed the consequences of an inevitable universal heat death and man's worldview in a famous 1903 passage:

> . . . Even more purposeless, more void of meaning, is the world which science presents for our belief. Amid such a world, if anywhere, our ideals henceforth must find a home. That man is the product of causes which have no prevision of the end they were achieving; that his origin, his growth, his hopes and fears, his loves and his beliefs, are but the outcome of accidental collocations of atoms; that no fire, no heroism, no intensity of thought and feeling, can preserve an individual life beyond the grave; that all the labors of the ages, all the devotion, all the inspiration, all the noonday brightness of human genius, are destined to extinction in the vast death of the solar system, and that the whole temple of man's achievement must inevitably be buried beneath the debris of a universe in ruins—all these things, if not quite beyond dispute, are yet so nearly certain that no philosophy which rejects them can hope to stand. Only within the scaffolding of these truths, *only on the firm foundation of unyielding despair,* can the soul's habitation henceforth be safely built [emphasis added].[19]

The view of this eminent philosopher is by no means isolated; this has been embraced as the quiet, noble burden-to-bear, willingly shouldered by those devoted to the secular notion of evolution. (i) **Naturalistic evolution reflects on no meaningful, lasting accomplishments.**

∎ ∎ ∎ ∎ ∎ ∎ ∎

With the naturalistic mindset and its insistence on internal conflict, it should come as no surprise that its insistence on disarray and hopelessness *can in no instance permit a view that offers hope, especially ultimate hope.* Since **evolution is not empirical** (that is, it cannot be proved with rigid and unbiased scientific procedures), it must hold an **imperial, exclusive** position. This is well illustrated by John Dunphy's militant humanism:

> The battle for humankind's future must be waged and won in the public school classroom by teachers who correctly perceive their role as the **proselytizers of a new faith:** a religion of humanity that recognizes and respects the spark of what theologians call divinity in every human being. These teachers must embody the same selfless dedication as the most rabid fundamentalist preachers, for they will be ministers of another sort, utilizing a classroom instead of a pulpit to convey humanist values in whatever subject they teach, regardless of the educational level—preschool, daycare, or large state university. The classroom must and will become an **arena of conflict** between the old and the new—the rotting corpse of Christianity, together with all its adjacent evils and misery, and the new faith of humanism, resplendent in its promise of a world in which the never-realized Christian ideal of "love thy neighbor" will finally be achieved [emphasis added].[20]

Has this policy actually been put into practice? Consider the admission of Dr. Lynn Margulis, who is recognized as a knowledgeable member of the "establishment":

> More and more . . . today's universities and professional societies guard their knowledge. Collusively, the university biology curriculum, the textbook publishers, the National Science Foundation review committees, the Graduate Record examiners, and the various microbiological, evolutionary, and zoological societies map out domains of the known and knowable; they distinguish required from forbidden knowledge, subtly punishing the trespassers with rejection and oblivion; they award the faithful liturgists by granting degrees and dispersing funds and fellowships. Universities and academies . . . determine who is permitted to know and just what it is that he or she may know. Biology, botany, zoology, biochemistry, and microbiology departments within the U.S. universities determine access to knowledge about life, dispensing it at high prices in peculiar parcels called credit hours.[21]

Michael Behe quotes philosopher Daniel Dennett as comparing religious believers (ninety percent of the population) to wild animals who may have to be caged. Dennett further says that parents should be prevented from misinforming their children about the "truth" of evolution.[22]

It follows naturally that the only way for evolution to triumph is to **remove the alternative**! In the minds of many the very definition of "science" has been rewritten to **exclude any interpretation** of universal history or life origin that suggests **supernatural intervention,**[23] no matter how overwhelmingly the evidence can be demonstrated. (j) **Naturalistic evolution permits no alternative.**

• • • • • • •

These "marks" of naturalistic philosophy are seen by many to be self-serving and reprehensible. Yet they are frequently held with earnest devotion, and in some instances cherished as a "badge of honor." What is the basis for such commitment? To find answers we are compelled to look further into the makeup of evolutionary dogma.

1. William Provine, "Influence of Darwin's Ideas on the Study of Evolution," *Science,* Vol. 32, June 1982, p. 506

2. Duane T. Gish, *Teaching Creation Science in Public Schools* (El Cajon, CA: Institute for Creation Research, 1995), p. 4

3. R. Lewontin, in the introduction to *Scientists Confront Creationism,* ed. L. R. Godfrey (New York: W. W. Norton and Co., 1983), p. xxvi.

4. Karl Popper, "Science: Problems, Aims, Responsibilities," *Proceedings,* Federation of American Society of Experimental Biology, Vol. 22 (1963), pp. 961–72.

5. L. Harrison Matthews, introduction to C. Darwin, *On the Origin of Species* (reprint, London: J. M. Dent and Sons, Ltd., 1971), p. XI

6. Sharon Begley, *Newsweek,* April 8, 1985, p. 80.

7. Michael Denton, *Evolution: A Theory in Crisis* (London: Burnett Books, 1985), p. 306

8. Hoyle, Sir Fred, and Chandra Wickramasinghe, *Evolution from Space* (New York: Simon and Schuster, 1984), p. 148

9. Leslie E. Orgel, "The Origin of Life on the Earth," *Scientific American,* Vol. 271, October 1994, p. 78

10. Raymond Eve, quoted by Janet Raloff, "When Science and Beliefs Collide," *Science News,* Vol. 149, June 8, 1996, p. 361

11. Carl Zimmer, "A Vision of the End," *Discover,* May 1993, p. 24.

12. Jeffrey Winters, "The Answer to the Voids," *Discover,* March 1996, p. 27

13. Stuart Wavel, "Is this proof that Darwin got it wrong?", *London Times,* October 13, 1996

14. Henry Morris, *Creation and the Modern Christian* (El Cajon: CA: Master Books Publishers, 1985), p. 91

15. Irving Stone, "The Death of Darwin," chapter 22 in *Darwin Up to Date,* ed. Jeremy Cherfas, (London: *New Scientist Guide,* IPC Magazines, Ltd., 1982), p. 69

16. Aldous Huxley, *Ends and Means* (New York: Harper and Brothers Publishers, 1937), pp. 312–16

17. James Rachels, *Created from Animals* (New York: Oxford Univer-

sity Press, 1990), p. 5

18. Charles Darwin, *Autobiography* (London: John Murray, 1860), p. 489

19. Bertrand Russell, 1957, pp. 106–7

20. John Dunphy, "A Religion for a New Age," *The Humanist*, Vol. 45, January/February 1983, p. 26

21. Lynn Margulis and Dorian Sagon, *Slanted Truths: Essays on Gaia, Symbiosis, and Evolution* (New York: Springer-Verlag, 1997), p. 265

22. Michael J. Behe, *Darwin's Black Box* (New York: The Free Press, 1996), p. 250, quoting Daniel Dennett, *Darwin's Dangerous Idea* (New York: Simon & Schuster, 1995), pp. 515–16

23. Sir Julian Huxley, "In the evolutionary system of thought there is no longer need or room for the supernatural," Associated Press dispatch, November 27, 1959

Chapter 2

Evolution Is Religious

The first historical reference to the concept of evolution is unquestionably **a religious context.** In this nonscientific, religious introduction to evolutionary ideas the earth was represented as developing out of chaos, naturally endowed with a *latent imminent potency*. The Babylonian religious document *Enuma elish* introduced these ideas, describing the world materializing as the offspring of a primordial mother and father (earth and sky). According to this Babylonian account the earth developed from chaos, introduced primitive life forms, and ultimately produced man.[1]

Expanding on these introductory ideas, the Greeks carried the torch of evolution to lofty pinnacles of naturalistic speculation. Henry Fairfield Osborn, the celebrated paleoanthropologist who supported the Scopes evolution trial, wrote:

> When I began the search for anticipations of the evolutionary theory . . . I was led back to the Greek natural philosophers and I was astonished to find how many of the pronounced and basic features of the Darwinian theory were anticipated even as far back as the seventh century B.C.[2]

A brief survey is in order. A cast of imposing characters

took center stage—entering, exiting, and reappearing by influence over a period of centuries. The first Greek naturalistic influence was **Anaximander** (c. 611–547 B.C.) who taught that man was derived from aquatic, fishlike mermen who emerged from the water after their bodies developed. He suggested that

> . . . the first animals were generated in the moisture, and were enclosed with spiny barks. As they grew older, they migrated onto the drier land; and once their bark was split and shed, they survived for a short time in the new mode of . . . existence.[3]

Some interesting elements were added to the concept by **Empedocles** (c. 490–430 B.C.). He also believed in a spontaneous generation of life, and postulated that the forces of love and hate playing on the four elements (earth, air, fire, water) produced the plants from which animals budded. Gerald Wheeler writes:

> Empedocles believed that originally the world contained creatures with every possible combination of limbs and other organs, since only parts of animals came into existence first. Hate for a time kept the parts separate, but love eventually allowed them to join at random. Modern species are those that survived after nature winnowed the odd assemblages out.[4]

Aristotle (384–322 B.C.) saw naturalistic progression in a slightly different light. To explain the fortunate components seen in nature he contended that

> . . . our teeth should come up *of necessity*—the front teeth sharp, fitted for tearing, the molars broad and use-

ful for grinding down the food—since they did not arise for this end, but it was merely a coincident result. . . . Wherever then all the parts came about just what they would have been if they had come to be for an end, such things survived, being organized spontaneously in a fitting way; whereas those which grew otherwise perished and continue to perish.[5]

Late in the first century B.C. the Greek historian **Diodoros** reverted back to fragments of Anaximander's ideas, as he reintroduced evolutionary mechanisms to a new generation. But the Romans preserved some of Aristotle's concepts. The Roman poet **Lucretius** (96?–55 B.C.) wrote about nature's elimination of mutants or deformed monsters and its preservation of beneficial traits:

. . . nor yet ever can things exist of twofold nature and double body, moulded into one from limbs of alien kind. . . . Each thing has its own process of growth; all must preserve their mutual differences, governed by Nature's irreversible law.[6]

This "law of nature" dominated the thinking of the ancients, where natural forces were thought to represent the rage of divine entities.

In general, myth conveys the impression of a story invented *ex nihilo*, a story describing the irascible and typically irresponsible actions of various divine malcontents. But these deities are not simply malevolent gods capriciously toying with mankind. They are actually personifications of Nature, and their activities, predictable and unpredictable, determine what life will be like on earth.[7]

The single exception to the practice of *deifying Nature* was the creation concept held by the Hebrews. John and Henry Morris demonstrate the naturalistic musings of the remaining ancients, in their attempts to explain the evolutionary origin and progression of life, to be religious to the core.[8]

Since such naturalistic musings could afford the luxury of unbridled speculation, evolution's modern hero, **Charles Darwin,** stretched far beyond the limits of empirical science in suggesting a means to accomplish the ends to which he was unalterably dedicated. Evolutionist Stephen Jay Gould quotes Darwin from the original edition of *Origins*, about a ridiculous explanation that was expunged in later issues:

> In North America the black bear was seen by Hearne swimming for hours with widely open mouth, thus catching, like a whale, insects in the water. . . . If the supply of insects were constant, and if better adapted competitors did not already exist in the country, I can see no difficulty in a race of bears being rendered, by natural selection, more and more aquatic in their structure and habits, with larger and larger mouths, till a creature was produced as monstrous as a whale.[9]

The reader should be aware of the fact that James B. Conant, former president of Harvard, defined science as ". . . an interconnected series of concepts and conceptual schemes that have developed as a result of **experimentation** and **observation.**"[10] In a supporting statement the *Harper Encyclopedia of Science* defines the scientific method as ". . . techniques of **controlled observation** employed in the search for knowledge."[11] Yet, modern evolutionary commitment has not learned much from

Darwin's rampant speculation. V. B. Scheffer related a rather imaginary tale in *National Geographic:*

> The whale's ascendancy to sovereign size apparently began sixty million years ago when hairy, four-legged mammals in search of food or sanctuary, ventured into water. As eons passed, changes slowly occurred. Hind legs disappeared, front legs changed into flippers, hair gave way to a thick smooth blanket of blubber, nostrils moved to the top of the head, the tail broadened into flukes, and in the buoyant water world, the body became enormous.[12]

France's leading zoologist, Pierre Grassé, cautioned: **"There is no law against daydreaming, but science must not indulge in it** [emphasis added]."[13]

But, indulge it does. Astrophysicists Li-Xin and J. Richard Gott III postulate that the universe actually created itself.[14] British astronomer and physicist Paul Davies believes that the creative cosmos has brought order from chaos:

> In recent years, more scientists have come to recognize that matter and energy possess an innate ability to self-organize. . . . [Note] the astonishing ability of an embryo to develop from a single strand of DNA, via an exquisitely well-organized sequence of formative steps, into an exceedingly complex organism.[15]

Evolutionist Rupert Sheldrake enlarges on the theme:

> All nature is evolutionary. The cosmos is like a great developing organism, and evolutionary creativity is inherent in nature herself. . . . The universe as a whole is a develop-

ing organism, and so are the galaxies, solar systems, and biospheres within it, including the earth.[16]

This speculative naturalistic worldview is not science and should not purport to be seen as such. It is, at the core, identification with **ancient pagan ideas:** "In fact, the belief that life had its origins in a single substance is so widespread among the various peoples of the world, primitive or civilized, that it can be considered one of the few universal themes in the history of ideas."[17]

But again, it is not science. Michael Ruse, in Britain's *New Scientist,* observed that:

> An increasing number of scientists, most particularly a growing number of evolutionists . . . argue that Darwinian evolutionary theory is **no genuine scientific theory at all**. . . . Many of the critics have the highest intellectual credentials [emphasis added].[18]

Sometimes open candor is exercised with reference to the theories on the origin of life. Authors Green and Goldberger note that ". . . the macromolecule-to-cell transition is a jump of fantastic dimensions, which lies beyond the range of testable hypothesis. **In this area all is conjecture** [emphasis added]."[19]

Professor Wolfgang Smith was educated at Cornell, Purdue, and Columbia, in physics and mathematics. His faculty positions include Oregon State, MIT, and UCLA. This qualified academician has substantiated his conclusions that the doctrine of macroevolution ". . . is **totally bereft of scientific sanction**. . . . [T]here exists to this day **not a shred of bona fide scientific evidence** in support of the thesis that macroevolutionary transformations have ever occurred."[20]

Yet, in spite of the fact that the concept is conjectural and bereft of scientific sanction, it is defended fiercely. This characteristic, too, identifies it with religious fervor. Philosopher Tom Bethell accurately describes the situation:

> Evolution is perhaps the most jealously guarded dogma of the American public philosophy. Any sign of serious resistance to it has encountered fierce hostility in the past, and it will not be abandoned without a tremendous fight. The gold standard could go, . . . the Constitution itself shyly junked. But Darwinism will be defended to the bitter end.[21]

The eminent British paleontologist, Colin Patterson, of the British Museum of Natural History, adequately assessed the broader scene. He appeared on a BBC radio program, in which he expressed some problems he had with evolutionary theory. In the BBC article describing the program this scholar is quoted as saying:

> Just as pre-Darwinian biology was carried out by people whose faith was in the Creator and His plan, post–Darwinian biology is being carried out by people whose faith is in, almost, **the deity of Darwin.** They've seen their task as to elaborate his theory and to fill the gaps in it. . . . But it seems to me that the theoretical framework has very little impact on the actual progress of the work in biological research. In a way some aspects of Darwinism and of neo-Darwinism seem to me to have **held back the progress of science** [emphasis added].[22]

Understanding the religious overtones inherent in evolutionary theory, we would do well to scan the list of major religions which embrace its tenets. Henry Morris of the Creation Research Institute has done this for us. He gives the following as a partial listing of those religions that are structured around an evolutionary philosophy:

Buddhism	Animism	Liberal Judaism
Hinduism	Spiritism	Liberal Islam
Confucianism	Occultism	Liberal Christianity
Taoism	Satanism	Unitarianism
Shintoism	Theosophy	Religious Science
Sikhism	Bahaism	Unity
Jainism	Mysticism	Humanism[23]

On the other hand, the list for modern creationist religions is quite short:

Orthodox Judaism
Orthodox Islam
Orthodox Christianity[24]

In order to properly assess the merits of each position, we need to proceed with definitions relating to the basic terms used. Wheeler offers a comprehensive **definition for evolution:**

> Most evolutionists postulate the spontaneous generation of life from nonliving materials at some time in the distant past. . . . All evolutionists visualize life as continually undergoing changes in physical form and behavior pattern because of external forces and random mutation of the genetic material. . . . All present life has descended from one or a few original forms.[25]

For the purpose of discussion, a distinction must be made between **microevolution** (the development of small changes or adaptations within genetic boundaries of an organism or population of organisms) and **macroevolution** (hypothetical development of beneficial changes beyond genetic boundaries, which would give rise to new organisms of a higher order). Creationists would agree that changes do occur within living systems. These changes (microevolution), however, are adaptations inherent within genetic boundaries. Where mutational changes exceed the original genetic boundaries, the results are detrimental and ultimately nonviable. They certainly do not lead to the development of higher life forms (macroevolution).

John Morris, director of the Creation Research Institute, provides a **definition for creation:** "Each basic category of life appeared abruptly, without descending from an ancestor of a different sort. Much variation within a category is expected, but each possessed genetic limits to its variability, and thus exhibited stasis."[26]

Duane Gish, associate director of the Creation Research Institute, has summarized the contrast between the two models:

Creation Model	**Evolution Model**
By acts of a Creator.	By naturalistic mechanistic processes due to properties inherent in inanimate matter.
Creation of basic plant and animal types with characteristics complete in first representatives.	Origin of all living things from a single living source which itself arose from inanimate matter. Origin of each kind from an ancestral form by slow gradual change.

Variation and speciation limited within each kind.	Unlimited variation. All forms genetically related.[27]

That same author then lists the predictions to be made by each model concerning the fossil record:

Creation Model	**Evolution Model**
Sudden appearance in great variety of highly complex forms.	Gradual change of simple forms into more and more complex forms.
Sudden appearance of each created type with characteristics complete.	Transitional series linking all categories.
Sharp boundaries separating major taxonomic groups. No transitional forms between higher categories.[28]	No systematic gaps.

The two models can be visualized on a large scale by the illustration on pages thirty-eight through forty-one.

Evolution has been championed by various devotees who have marched under its banner with abandon. In our modern era its propelling process was first claimed to be *acquired characteristics*, then *survival of the fittest*, followed by *crossbreeding*, to be replaced by *micro–mutations*, and now supplanted by *punctuated equilibrium*. Each new approach to the problems presented by scientific investigation affirms that the previous ideas were tacitly wrong! Yet it continues to be supported with unswerving dedication. Such vacillation, while adhering to its cherished dogma, unmasks the religious inheritance of the theory as a belief system. Its modern hero practiced the same, as author Jacques Barzun indicates.

Darwin was not a thinker and he did not originate the ideas that he used. He vacillated, added, retracted, and confused his own traces. As soon as he crossed the dividing line between the realm of events and the realm of theory he became "metaphysical" in the bad sense.[29]

Jonathan Howard is a principal scientific officer at the ARC Institute of Animal Physiology at Babraham, England. He candidly wrote: "With the centenary of Dar-win's death comes a widespread mood of scepticism and unease about the validity and significance of Darwin's contribution to knowledge."[30]

Two medical researchers from the University of Iowa have recently re-diagnosed the ills of Charles Darwin. Barloon and Noyes describe Darwin as possessing at least nine of the thirteen classic symptoms for panic disorder listed in standard physicians reference. According to these researchers the conditions viewed as a whole make *an overwhelming case for phobic panic disorder*. Darwin complained of being "unwell, with a swimming of the head, depression and trembling." He wrote to a friend that "anything which flurries me . . . brings on violent palpitations of the heart." The anxiety he felt after speaking at the Linnaean Society in London brought on twenty-four hours of vomiting. Ultimately he left his home only in the company of his wife, and rarely at that.[31] Could it be that his theories are inseparably linked with a phobic response to explanations involving the material universe?

One characteristic that places this dogma in the religious category is that its basic tenets cannot be "proved" in a final sense. They must ultimately be taken on faith. A 1997 National Science Teachers Association survey showed twenty-three percent of the science teachers strongly agreeing that evolution is a scientific fact, with twenty-eight percent strongly disagreeing that it is a scientific fact. Fourteen percent strongly believed that life evolved from a simple cell to more complex organisms,

ENERGY TO MATTER
CREATOR EXPRESSES LIGHT/ENERGY

JACK HAMM

BIG BANG THEORY - Timeline of th

Atoms form from energy of light, later to be cooked to heavier elements in stars, ultimately to provide the material out of which life would arise.

GRAVITY

ELECTRO MAGNETISM

MATTER/RADIATION

END OF NUCLEOSYSTHESIS

WEAK FORCE

STRONG FORCE

PROTONS & NEUTRONS

MOMENT OF INFINITE TEMPERATURE

ERA OF INFLATION
10^{12} SECOND

10^{1} SECOND

10^{1} SECONDS

while twenty-seven percent strongly disagreed.[32]

The general public assumes that scientists "have their act together"—that evolutionary theorists have worked

Immediately Materialized in Universal Design

Universe

**UNIVERSE
BECOMES
TRANSPARENT
(ORIGIN OF THE
MICROWAVE
BACKGROUND)**

**GALAXIES
AND
QUASARS APPEAR**

**CURRENT CHAOTIC
UNIVERSE BECOMES
SELF-REALIZING
IN THE MIND OF MAN**

300,000 YEARS   ONE BILLION YEARS   15 BILLION YEARS

Non-Living
Material

Illustration of "MORPHING" Techniqu

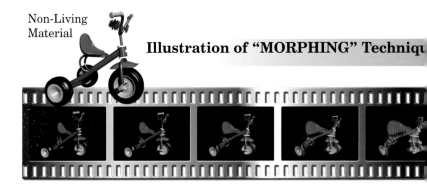

out all the kinks. Nothing could be further from the truth. To underscore the fact that there is **no real scientific consensus** on universal explanations, Michael Duff, writing in *Scientific American,* stated

> . . . it is worth emphasizing that the two main pillars of twentieth century physics, quantum mechanics and Einstein's general theory of relativity, are mutually incompatible. General relativity fails to comply with the quantum rules that govern the behavior of elementary particles, whereas on the opposite scale, black holes are challenging the very foundations of quantum mechanics. *Something big has to give.*[33]

It is the considered opinion of this researcher that the theory of evolution itself is seriously straddled with haunting dilemmas. Its primary academic assumptions are incompatible with results of scientific research, which were designed to prove its validity. Every attempt at novel explanations adds to the list of untenable hypotheses and raises the theory to a new level of uncertainty. Since it is inherently religious in its very nature and is bereft of scientific verification, the theory is useless in its explanatory value.

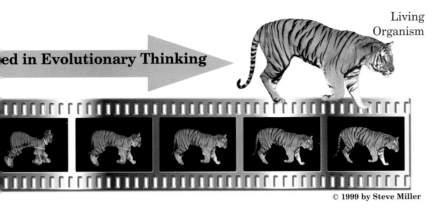

Living
Organism

ed in **Evolutionary Thinking**

© 1999 by Steve Miller

Why, then, is it taught as a tenable theory, and in many instances as established fact? One reason is that man is very good at a "mind game" called **morphing.** To "morph" is defined as "to change forms." This ability to "daydream" and *envision something which is not really true* makes for a normal, healthy imagination (as long as we know the difference between our daydreams and current reality!).

Actually, it requires a fair amount of intelligence (and ability at conceptualizing) to envision an entity in a form (or state) other than it now appears. Human nature is then susceptible to taking pride in designing a creative scenario, especially if the idea had not occurred to others. An additional susceptibility to pride occurs when one is able to "grasp" the creative idea that another person has constructed. This is increasingly true if the efforts reach a common goal—such as envisioning how life could have come about. It naturally follows that others who do not embrace the concept are often considered less "intellectual," as if they were not quite bright enough to comprehend an advanced algebraic concept. It may be, instead, that the unresponsive person is actually able to discern reality from fantasy to a higher degree!

An illustration can be given of morphing a *tricycle*

into a *tiger*. We can envision various changing steps as the child's mechanical toy develops into a pulsating cat, gracefully enjoying its surroundings. This generates excellent material for make-believe cartoons, but it hardly qualifies as a candidate for reality.

*The theory of evolution is an **exercise in morphing**, and morphing is in essence an **exercise in faith**.* In some instances an unrestrained imagination can envision how a change from one structure to another might occur. In other instances there is not even an imaginary series of steps that can be envisioned to accomplish the desired alteration. In addition, if these imaginary steps actually violate experimental laboratory data, we have proceeded from the "desired" to the "ludicrous."

By proceeding from *desiring the validity of a concept* to *assuming the reality of each imaginary phase required to materialize the concept*, the proponents of evolutionary philosophy have underscored the religious nature of the theory. As was noted earlier in this chapter, Darwin "crossed the dividing line between the realm of events and the realm of theory."[34] He denied the tenets of one religion (Christianity), only to don the tapestry of his own religious exercise!

Scientist John Little admitted: "Evolution is the creation myth of our age. . . . A belief in evolution is a religion in itself."[35]

Historian Marjorie Grene stated: "It is as a religion of science that Darwinism chiefly held, and holds men's minds."[36]

Physics professor H. S. Lipson at the University of Manchester observed: "In fact, evolution became, in a sense, a scientific religion; almost all scientists have accepted it and many are prepared to 'bend' their observations to fit in with it."[37]

Chandra Wickramasinghe, in his testimony at the Arkansas Balanced Treatment case, December 1981, gave the following sweeping assessment:

> Contrary to the popular notion that only creationism relies on the supernatural, evolutionism must as well, since the probabilities of the random formation of life are so tiny as to require a "miracle" for spontaneous generation to have occurred, making belief in spontaneous generation "tantamount to a theological argument."[38]

The *Humanist Manifesto* lists evolution as its primary dogma.[39] In 1961 the Supreme Court of the United States recognized humanism to be religious in nature.[40] Professor L. H. Matthews, a well-recognized evolutionist, wrote a new introduction for the 1971 edition of Darwin's *Origin of Species*. In this introduction he admitted: "Most biologists accept it (i.e. evolution) as though it were a proven fact, although this conviction rests upon circumstantial evidence, it forms a satisfactory **faith** on which to base our interpretation of nature [emphasis added]."[41]

1. *Encyclopedia Britannica*, "Doctrines and Dogmas, Religious," 1990, vol. 17, p. 369
2. Henry Fairfield Osborn, *From the Greeks to Darwin* (New York: Charles Scribner's Sons, 1929), p. xi
3. Quoted in Stephen Toulmin and June Goodfield, *The Discovery of Time* (New York: Harper & Row, Publishers, 1965), p. 36
4. Gerald W. Wheeler, *The Two-Tailed Dinosaur* (Nashville: Southern Publishing Association, 1975), p. 23
5. Aristotle, *Physica*, R. P. Hardie and R. K. Gaye, trans. *The Works of Aristotle*, Vol. II (Oxford: Clarendon Press, 1930), p. 198
6. Lucretius, *De Rerem Natura*, R. C. Trevelyan, trans. (Cambridge: Cambridge University Press, 1937), pp. 209, 211
7. Ernest L. Abel, *Ancient Views on the Origin of Life* (Fairleigh Dickinson University Press, 1973), p. 15
8. Henry M. Morris and John D. Morris, "Society and Creation, The Long History of Evolution," *The Modern Creation Trilogy* (Green Forest, AR: Master Books, 1996), p. 47

9. Stephen Jay Gould, *Natural History*, "Full of Hot Air," October 1989, p. 28

10. James B. Conant, quoted by Frank Sherwin, *ICR Impact Series*, "Inspired Guesses, Creative Imagination, and Science," (El Cajon, CA: Institute for Creation Research), Feb. 1998, p. a

11. Ibid., p. a

12. Ibid., p. b

13. Pierre Grassé, *Evolution of Living Organisms*, 1997, p. 103

14. Li-Xin and J. Richard Gott III, "Evading Quantum Barrier to Time Travel," *Science News*, April 11, 1998, p. 231

15. Paul Davies, "The Creative Cosmos," *New Scientist*, Vol. 116, December 17, 1987, p. 42

16. Rupert Sheldrake, *The Rebirth of Nature: The Greening of Science and of God* (New York: Bantam Books, 1991), pp. 95,151

17. Ernest L. Abel, *Ancient Views on the Origin of Life* (Fairleigh Dickinson University Press, 1973), p. 15

18. Michael Ruse, "Darwin's Theory: An Exercise in Science," *New Scientist*, June 25, 1981, p. 828

19. D. E. Green and R. F. Goldberger, *Molecular Insights into the Living Process* (New York: Academic Press, 1967), p. 407

20. Wolfgang Smith, *Teilhardism and the New Religion*, Tan Books, 1988, pp. 5,6

21. Tom Bethell, *The American Spectator*, July 1994, p. 17

22. Leith, *The Listener,* 106:390 (1981).

23. Henry M. Morris, *What Is Creation Science?* (El Cajon: CA, Master Books, 1987), p. 17

24. Ibid., p. 20

25. Wheeler, op. cit., pp. 19–20

26. John D. Morris, *The Young Earth* (Green Forest, AR: Master Books, 1997), p. 10

27. Duane T. Gish, *Evolution: The Fossils Still Say NO!* (El Cajon, CA: Institute for Creation Research, 1995), p. 42

28. Ibid., p. 43

29. Jacques Barzun, *Darwin, Marx, Wagner,* 2nd ed. (Garden City, NY: Doubleday and Co., 1959), p. 84

30. Jonathan Howard, *Darwin* (Oxford University Press), preface

31. Thomas Barloon and Russel Noyes, "On the Origin of Darwin's Ills," *Discover,* September 1997, p. 27

32. Richard Overman and Steve Deckard, "Origins Belief Among NSTA Members," *Impact*, Institute for Creation Research, El Cajon: CA

33. Michael J. Duff, "The Theory Formerly Known as Strings," *Scientific American*, February 1998, p. 64

34. Jacques Barzun, op. cit.

35. John Little, "When Scientists Are Unscientific," *New Scientist*, 109 (1986), pp. 50,51

36. Marjorie Grene, *Encounter,* November 1959, p. 48.
37. H. S. Lipson, "A Physicist Looks at Evolution," *Physics Bulletin*, Vol. 31 (1980)
38. Chandra Wickramasinghe, testimony in the Arkansas Balanced Treatment case, December 1981, cited in Bill Keith, *Scopes II: The Great Debate* (Shreveport, LA: Huntington House, 1982), p. 137
39. Humanist Manifesto II, *The Humanist*, September/October 1973, Vol. XXXIII, No. 5
40. Supreme Court of the United States: *Torcaso v. Watkins*, 367 IJS 488 (1961), footnote 11, p. 495
41. L. H. Matthews, introduction to 1971 edition of Darwin's *Origin of Species*

Chapter 3

Universal Physics

Origin and *development* of the known universe are necessary topics for discussion in explaining the existence of what we see around us. Credible scientific explanations would be in order if an attempt were made to justify supposed evolutionary processes for what we find. Under close scrutiny these so-called "scientific explanations"[1] take on bizarre details, requiring undiscovered organizing principles over and above the known laws of physics.[2] These assumptions need to be explored.

The current explanation for the natural *origin* and development of the universe postulates: (1) by "closed time loops" *the universe created itself.*[3] During that initial event (2) a "special kind of symmetry" held sway, and the forces of nature were indistinguishable. The incalculable energy available would (3) "endow" the infant cosmos with a "kind of antigravity" to provide a repulsive force. This *inflation theory* further postulates that (4) "in less than a trillionth of a trillionth of a second, the cosmos ballooned from a radius one-millionth the size of a proton to literally cosmic proportions."[4] Microscopic ripples in space (5) evolved into "underdensities" and "overdensities" in mass that could then be molded by gravity into our present-day universe. At the outset the universe was a mixture of radiation, electrons, and ions; then the universe cooled enough for subatomic particles to combine into atoms.[5] (6) The original temperature was infinite, but at this point the infant universe cooled enough for us to apply modern physical theories. Matter was formed slightly in excess of antimatter, and (7) an exotic type of "cold dark matter" was produced to maintain critical density. (8) Galaxies were formed, and stars "cooked" the heavier elements into existence.[6] From those original natural conditions (9) life arose on planet Earth, and as its ultimate product we are here to ponder its mysteries!

Is there even the slightest thread of evidence that any of this took place? Not only is there *no scientific evidence that any of this occurred*; there is a body of scientific data insisting that ***it could not have occurred***. The technical literature is written with a "given" that evolution *has* occurred; we are simply in the ever-mystifying process of guessing *how* it occurred. The scenario reflected above is composed of arbitrary conditions, imposed by "morphing" ideas in order to arrive at a desired naturalistic explanation. Yet, the elements of the concept are irreconcilable with each other.

The following reference outlines and underscores the irreconcilable nature of these elements, author Steven Weinberg wrote in *Scientific American*:

> If we try to write down some dynamical equations that will automatically give results consistent with some of these conditions, we usually find that *the results violate the other conditions* [emphasis added]. . . . We cannot resolve these problems by requiring that all experiments should give sensible results. . . . Life as we know it would be impossible if any one of several physical quantities has slightly different values.[7]

This inability to reconcile the elements of the paradigm is, however, endemic to the mindset of evolution: it is by its own nature a phobic preoccupation *which will permit no ultimate answers* (see chapter ten). To Charles Darwin the chaos of his mind was corollary with his theories, and the modern adherents often display kindred attitudes in emotional response and in the theories they embrace. This assessment is not offered as harsh criticism, but as compassionate understanding of the unsatisfied turmoil experienced by an evolutionary mindset.

The reader should not be intimidated by the apparent sophistication of the arguments for evolutionary origins. In the *Scientific American* article mentioned above, very telling admissions expose the **speculative nature** of the naturalistic explanation: "it is generally assumed"; "we cannot directly observe"; "even in its simplest form it contains a number of arbitrary features"; "it has been conjectured that"; "if this is true"; "these ideas will remain speculative"; "it is not yet definitely solved."[8]

Since it is not yet definitely solved, let us deal with the basic pillars of this "Big Bang" inflationary hypothesis under **scientific scrutiny.** In the *Scientific American* special issue cited above, respected authors define work in this area: "[T]here are certainly unresolved issues within the theory itself. . . . In science, we adopt the plodding route: we accept only what is tested by *experimentation* or *observation*."[9]

Since there are unresolved issues within the theory itself, we shall proceed to deal with the basic increments —and accept only what is tested by experimentation or observation. Let's examine them briefly in the order they were introduced.

Hypothesis	*Objection*:
"The universe created itself	Stephen Hawking objects, stating stating that **physical laws**

in closed time loops." ***do not permit*** the appearance of closed timelike curves.[10] In suggesting that "the laws of physics may allow the universe to be its own mother"[11] these authors have ventured beyond the "cause and effect" physics of reality. Some theoretical astronomers suggest that modern cosmology "has left the world of physics behind" to enter "the realm of metaphysics."[12]

"A special kind of symmetry held sway and the forces of nature were indistinguishable."

This *ad hoc* explanation **suspends the laws of nature** and envisions a "make believe" condition totally contrary to the physics of the universe.[13] Stephen Weinberg was well advised in admitting "we are led at last to laws of nature that **cannot be explained within the boundaries of contemporary science**. . . . A further complex of puzzles overhangs the laws of nature and the initial conditions."[14] This suspension of universal laws renders the concept void of scientific merit.

"The infant cosmos was 'endowed' with a kind of 'antigravity' to provide a repulforce."

Such "endowment" is nothing more than wishful supposition." Weinberg again admits, "We do not have enough confidence in sive the application of these laws at extreme temperatures and densities to be sure that there really was such a moment, much less to work out all the initial conditions, **if there were any.**"[15]

"In less than a trillionth of a trillionth of a second the cosmos ballooned from a radius of one-millionth the size of a proton to cosmic proportions."

Infinite velocity is "invoked" for universal radiation. If such velocity occurred it would decay to its current 186,282.0244866 miles-per-second rate of speed. Such decay would follow a predictable line, such as an "exponentially damped sinusoidal curve." This decay rate would render the age of the universe in thousands of years, and thus nullify any evolutionary explanation.

"Evolved into 'under-densities' and 'over-densities' in mass that could then be molded by gravity into our present-day universe."

Notice that the universe is conveniently "endowed" with gravity in order to affect mass at a pre cise moment. To support this idea, evolutionary physicists have postulated that the universe is ninety-five percent composed of some "exotic type material that doesn't emit light and can't be seen."[16] This phantom material is dubbed "cold dark matter," and it has never been found. To the **embarrassment of the theory** "myriad studies suggest that the density of the universe is considerably less than the critical density"[17] required for its support. Additionally, the theory predicts much more clustering of galaxies than astronomers observe.[18]

"Temperature was infinite . . . cooled to apply modern physitheories."

We have already seen that Weinberg holds no confidence in temperatures and densities at cal this extreme and is forced to write that there may not have been such an event at all.[19] Modern physical theories are **arbitrarily inserted** as a "convenient endowment."

"Cold dark matter produced."

This subject was covered in was point five since it is related to the "missing mass" of the universe. "The realization that we still do not know what makes up most of the universe has thrown astronomy off the track of normal science and into a crisis."[20]

"Galaxies formed and stars produced heavier elements."

Evolutionary theory on formation of galaxies is contradictory. "We know of no process that can maintain a spiral arm for more than two galactic revolutions."[21] "If his theory is true, the universe is young, since it has so many rapidly revolving spirals."[22] "Data from the Hubble telescope . . . call physicists' cherished theories into question."[23] "The process by which galaxies clump together poses a **significant mystery** for astronomers."[24]

"Life arose on planet Earth."

"The likelihood of the formation of life from inanimate matter is one to a number with 40,000 noughts after it. . . . It is big enough to bury Darwin and the whole theory of evolution. There was no primeval soup, neither on this planet nor on any other, and if the beginnings of life were not random, they must therefore have been the product of purposeful intelligence."[25] DNA expert Francis Crick agrees there is virtually **no chance that the first life could have spontaneously generated from Earth's chemistry.**[26]

"Man is evolution's ultimate product."

The astonishingly large number of possible interconnections within the human brain far exceed the number of atoms in the entire physical universe.[27] Man and his brain are **unique creations.**[28] "Any attempt to promote this [human evolution] theory as reasonable and valid in light of so many discrepancies seems deceptive or duplicitous."[29]

)Many serious students of evolutionary theory, both those supporting its basic concepts and those disavowing its scientific validity, have voiced hesitation regarding its plausibility. An example of that hesitation was published in *Nature*: "There is no mechanism known as yet that would allow the universe to begin in an arbitrary state and then evolve to its present highly-ordered state."[30]

Quasars, redshifts, and astronomical distances are a part of the controversy surrounding the origin of the universe. Astronomer Halton Arp published *Quasars, Redshifts and Controversies*. For twenty-nine years he was a staff astronomer at the facilities known originally as the Mt. Wilson and Palomar Observatories. After examination of the fundamental data, this accredited scholar has concluded that:

> Far from being the most distant objects in the universe, quasars are associated in space with relatively nearby galaxies. . . . Quasars' enormous redshifts do *not* arise from the expansion of the universe, but rather are intrinsic properties of the quasars themselves. . . . Quasars and galaxies have an origin far different from that assumed in the "standard" big-bang model of the universe.[31]

Sam Flamsteed, writing in *Discover* magazine, probably made a slight overstatement, but his point is well taken. He wrote:

> A good astronomical theorist never lets the complete absence of information stand in the way of a nice theory and, conversely, never gets thrown when an actual observation arrives to spoil it. Lack of data can actually be an advantage. Unhindered by facts, some theorist is bound

to have come up with a model that explains even the strangest discovery.[32]

A growing number of accredited scientists are taking a hard look at the facts. They are to be commended for adopting a more objective approach. British physicist H. S. Lipson expressed his interest in life's origin in a very candid manner:

> Evolution became in a sense a scientific religion; almost all scientists have accepted it and many are prepared to "bend" their observations to fit with it. . . . To my mind, the theory [evolution] does not stand up at all. . . . If living matter is not, then, caused by the interplay of atoms, natural forces, and radiation, how has it come into being? . . . I think, however, that we must go further than this and admit that the only acceptable explanation is **creation** [emphasis his].[33]

Evolution won't work in the light of universal physics. Additionally, the theory is lacking in scientific validity because of . . .

1. Donald Goldsmith, "The Fingerprint of Creation, *Discover*, October 1992, pp. 74–84

2. Paul Davies, *The Cosmic Blueprint* (New York: Simon and Schuster, 1988), p. 142

3. Li-Xin and J. Richard Gott III, "Evading Quantum Barrier to Time Travel," *Science News*, April 11, 1998. p. 231

4. Ron Cowen, reporting theory proposed by Alan H. Guth, "From Soup to Us," *Science News*, Vol. 151, June 7, 1997, p. 354

5. Ibid., p. 355

6. Steven Weinberg, "Life in the Universe," *Scientific American*, October 1994, p. 45

7. Ibid., pp. 48,49

8. Ibid., pp. 46–48

9. P. James, E. Peeples, David N. Schramm, Edwin L. Turner, Richard G. Kron, "The Evolution of the Universe," *Scientific American*, October 1994, p. 53

10. *Science News*, Vol. 153, April 11, 1998, p. 231
11. Li-Xin and J. Richard Gott III, op. cit.
12. Tony Rothman and George Ellis, "Has Cosmology Become Metaphysical?" *Astronomy*, February 1987, pp. 6–22
13. James Ganz, "Which Way to the Big Bang?" *Science*, vol. 284, May 28, 1999, p. 1448.
14. Stephen Weinberg, op. cit., p. 45
15. Ibid.
16. Ron Cowan, op. cit., p. 354
17. Ibid., p. 355
18. Ibid.
19. Stephen Weinberg, op. cit.
20. Carlos Frenk and Simon White, "More Missing Matter Mystery," *Nature*, Vol. 317, October 24, 1985, p. 671
21. Hadley Wood, *Unveiling the Universe* (New York: American Elsevier Publishing Company, 1968), p. 188
22. C. B. Clason, *Exploring the Distant Stars* (New York: G. P. Putnam's Sons, 1958), p. 326
23. Michael D. Lemonick, "Oops . . . Wrong Answer," *Time*, November 7, 1994, p. 69
24. Jay Gallagher and Jean Keppel, "Seven Mysteries of Galaxies," *Astronomy*, Vol. 22, March 1994, p. 41
25. Frederick Hoyle, "Hoyle on Evolution," *Nature*, Vol. 294, No. 5837, November 12, 1981, p. 148
26. Francis Crick, *Life Itself* (New York: Simon and Schuster, 1981), pp. 117–41
27. C. Judson Herrick, *Brains of Rats and Man: A Survey of the Origin and Biological Significance of the Cerebral Cortex* (New York: Hafner Publishing Co., 1963), p. 382
28. Kevin C. McLeod, "Studying the Human Brain," *Creation Research Society Quarterly*, Vol. 20, No. 2, September 1983, pp. 75–79
29. Mark Dwinell, "Molecular Evolution or Bust," *Origins Research*, Vol. 8, No. 2, p. 11
30. Don N. Page, "Inflation Does Not Explain Time Asymmetry," *Nature*, Vol. 304, July 7, 1983, p. 40
31. Halton Arp, *Quasars, Redshifts and Controversies* (Berkeley: CA, Interstellar Media, 1987)
32. Sam Flamsteed, "Impossible Planets," *Discover*, September 1997, p. 81
33. H. S. Lipson, "A Physicist Looks at Evolution," *Physics Bulletin*, May 1980, p. 138

Chapter 4

The Origin of Life

Earlier in this text the reader was introduced to the concept of "morphing." This creative "mind game" was never more apparent than in the illusory "road to life" supposedly taken by simple inorganic chemistry evolving into complicated living systems.

The envisioned epoch is graphically portrayed in breathtaking drama, as we watch each scene unfold and anticipate subsequent developments with cliffhanging suspense. It is not difficult to get caught up in emotional identification with blobs of gooey compounds venturing into uncharted waters through eons of time, ultimately parading in unashamed dignity as man—the master of his own destiny. Writing in a popular magazine, George Alexander tells the story rather convincingly:

> Four billion years ago, the young planet was a hellish place. Volcanoes were everywhere, chuffing gases, water vapor, and blobs of lava. The gloomy skies, only here and there pierced by shafts of strong sunlight, were frequently illuminated by lightning strikes and the glare of volcanic eruptions. There was no sea, no land, no life. Earth, then only 500 million years old, was still warm; its crust was thin and brittle as the crackling skin of a roasted turkey. That thin veneer heaved and shuttered from the turbulence of the molten matter sloshing just underneath.

But all this changed in just a few hundred million years. The outermost layers of Earth cooled and thickened, snuffing out the volcanoes. Water vapor in the air condensed and fell to the surface as rain, collecting in the numerous low-lying craters.

Act I was over and Act II was about to begin, an act that would build to a wonderful climax: Life.

When did life begin? . . . Single-celled creatures similar to bacteria were building reeflike rocks in the shallow waters of lagoons as far back as 3.5 billion years ago. Rockbuilding is something that only a relatively advanced creature could do, so from this we infer that simple creatures, ancestral to these, had to exist as far back as 3.8 billion years, maybe 4 billion years. This takes us back almost to earth's beginning—as if life were somehow inherent in matter and the evolution of planets.

. . . Back in the 1920s, Alexander Oparin, a Russian, and J. B. S. Haldane, a Briton, independently proposed the first detailed sequences whereby life could have emerged from non-living chemicals reacting together on primitive Earth. Haldane pondered the vigorous chemistry that cosmic rays, lightning, and volcanoes would produce in those days, and concluded that "organic" (that is, carbon-based) molecules would easily have formed under such conditions. Ultimately washed into the oceans by rivers and streams, these molecules would have accumulated and given the early oceans the consistency of a warm, rich broth.

Oparin also focused on the chemical richness of the early oceans, speculating that the first cells would have been sticky, floating bubbles called gel droplets. As they exchanged chemicals with the sea around them, gel droplets would eventually assemble *self-replicating* molecules.

. . . Recent experiments have corroborated that mineral sheets of clay will concentrate organic molecules in a finely confined volume as water evaporates, orient them in ways that would facilitate linkups with other molecules, and shield the fragile, newly formed compounds from destructive solar radiation. Scientists have also used clays as catalysts to build short strings of amino acids—a first step toward fashioning the very long chains of amino acids that we know as proteins.

. . . Thus life, once begun, began to change—as in the symbiotic partnerships of different bacterial types to start what eventually became the animal, plant, and fungi kingdoms of today. But the most dramatic event of all was the primordial advance from non-life to life, which apparently took place in the sun-baked clays of ocean beaches.[1]

In another popular periodical renowned scientists give variations of the same theme. Harvard astronomer Patrick Thaddeus muses, "My guess is that almost everything is there [in space] at some level. I'm prepared to believe almost any reasonable molecule can be made in space."[2] Astrophysicist Mayo Greenberg adds, "These complex organics are undoubtedly of prebiological significance."[3] Martin Marietta astronomer Ben Clark concludes, "It could be that the origin of life depended on interstellar processes. That would mean we really were star men."[4] The scenario of their "road to life" is outlined as follows:

It is long, and it has four stages. First, simple molecules (1) made of atoms of carbon, hydrogen, oxygen, and nitrogen must react to produce biological monomers. (2) The monomers then form the three key components of a living cell: proteins, nucleic acids (DNA), and lipids. (3) A protein chain may have hundreds of amino-acid links; millions of nucleotides may be strung together to make a DNA double helix. In a living cell (4), lipids and proteins form the outer membrane, proteins catalyze all chemical reactions, and DNA (the stuff of genes) directs the show.[5]

A simplified diagram is shown here.

© 1999 by Steve Miller

Looking beyond the emotionally charged eloquence with which the scene has been described, we are obligated to apply rigorous scrutiny to the details in question. After all, the theme we are discussing is our own heritage!

David Skjaerlund published a penetrating article in *Destiny*. Among other things his insightful research revealed:

The origin of life from nonlife through natural processes and its subsequent evolution of species depends on the right events occurring at the right time. Upon closer examination of the natural processes, the odds of life originating by chance become infinitesimally small and improbable.[6]

As we shall see, the odds of producing life by natural processes are *virtually impossible*. Sir Frederick Hoyle posited that those who hold to this impossible scenario "believe in a miracle somewhere in the laws of the universe."[7] Author Skjaerlund continued by explaining the intricate steps required to produce living systems.

The origin of life by natural processes would involve the following steps:

1. formation of simple building blocks such as proteins and nucleic acids;
2. arrangement of these molecules into biologically important compounds such as proteins and DNA;
3. assembly of these proteins into a metabolically active system, and [organization] of the first completely independent, stable and self-replicating cell;
4. [initiation of] drastic changes in the genetic material to produce completely different types and forms of life.[8]

Skjaerlund then details why this is beyond the realm of the possible.

Most of the cell's important functions are carried out by compounds called proteins which are a chain of amino acids (twenty different types) linked together. The protein's characteristics and functions are determined by the number and particular arrangement of amino acids. An appropriate analogy of a protein is a sentence, which derives its meaning from the particular arrangement of letters and words.

. . . Amino acids . . . can exist in two forms which have the same chemical composition but are three dimensional mirror images of each other; thus termed right and left handed amino acids or isomers. . . . Every protein in a living cell uniquely consists entirely of left handed amino acids, even though the right handed isomer can react in the same way and nature cannot distinguish the two isomers.

. . . Some basic amino acids and nucleic acids have been formed [in laboratory experiments] but have not been anything closely resembling a living cell. . . . The products from the "primordial soup" experiments have been a mixture of a few right and left handed amino acids . . . result[ing] in approximately fifty percent of each.

However, we are faced with an even greater dilemma. Proteins are functional because the amino acids arranged in a specific sequence, not just a random arrangement of left handed amino acids. . . . What is the probability then of synthesizing proteins with a specific sequence? Let us simplify the situation first. For example, if there are seventeen students in a class, how many possible ways exist for them to order themselves in a line? . . . [T]here are over 355 trillion ways. If the number of students is increased to twenty [the same number of amino acid types linked together to form proteins], . . . the number of possible ways would equal the number of seconds in 4.5 billion years.

The probability [problem] is even greater when one considers there are twenty possibilities for each spot and each protein consists of hundreds of amino acids linked together in a *very specific* sequence to determine the function of that protein. . . . If only one amino acid is changed . . . [malfunction] results. . . . Hundreds of proteins are required for even the most basic functions of the simplest living organisms.[9]

Skjaerlund then quotes from biochemist Michael Denton (*Evolution: A Theory in Crisis*) regarding even the simplest of living cells:

In effect it is a veritable micro-miniaturized factory containing thousands of exquisitely designed pieces of intricate molecular machinery, made up of one hundred thousand million atoms, far more complicated than any machine built by man and absolutely without parallel in the non living world.[10]

Within the past few decades molecular researchers have made much of the experiments performed by Stanley Miller. A diagram of the famous apparatus is shown below.

As authors Richard B. Bliss, Gary E. Parker, and Duane T. Gish point out, the trivial nature of these results cannot be ignored:

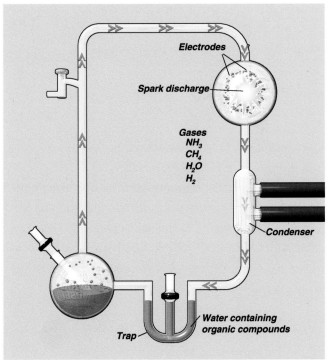

© 1999 by Steve Miller

All that were produced in these experiments were a few amino acids and other very simple compounds. The origin of life would require the production of *all* the amino acids, sugars, purines, pyrimidines, and other compounds, and their combination in the macromolecules, such as proteins, carbohydrates, DNA, and RNA, as well as the construction of the exceedingly complex, self-replicating cell.

A vital part of Miller's apparatus is a *cold trap* to collect the products as they were formed from chemical reactions. Actually, without this trap, the chemical products would have been destroyed by the energy source (electrical sparking). It is important for us to realize that the energy which forms the molecules is also the energy that *destroys* these molecules as they are formed.[11]

A highly acclaimed research project on this question of natural chemical evolution concluded:

The law of mass action . . . predicts that any concentrating mechanisms (such as freezing or evaporating ponds) would merely have served to accelerate *both* destructive and synthetic processes already going on at slower rates in the dilute seas. In the end there would have been no discernible chemical evolutionary benefit from these small concentrating ponds. . . . It was both a lack of sufficient energy mobilizing means to harness the energy to the specific task of building biopolymers and a lack of means to generate the proper sequence . . . to get biological function.

Here the difficulty is fundamental. It applies equally to discarded, present, and possible future models of chemical evolution. . . . So-called protocells have been produced in the laboratory in an attempt to bridge the nonliving and the living. Such structures do have the crude resemblance to true cells but none of the internal cellular machinery, such as enzymes, DNA, or phospholipid cell membranes. The few "cell" functions manifested by protocell systems typically arise from simple physical forces. Any similarity to true cellular processes is highly superficial.

The advance of science itself is what is challenging the notion that life arose on earth by spontaneous . . . chemical reactions.[12]

Perhaps the reader is beginning to realize the enormity of the dilemma facing an evolutionary explanation for life's origins. Biochemist Duane Gish puts the problem in proper perspective:

By adding up the energy content of all the chemical bonds in a "simple" bacterium and comparing this to the energy content at equilibrium of the constituent atoms from which it was formed, Morowitz calculated the probability of this cell to be . . . one chance out of a number formed by writing the number followed by 100 billion zeroes! . . . Are there natural forces at work that could enable this monstrous improbability to be overcome? Of course not.[13] [Any odds beyond 1 in 10^{50} has zero probability of ever happening!][14]

Evolutionist Andrew Scott, writing in *New Scientist*, punctuated the point of our discussion:

But how much of this neat tale is firmly established, and how much remains hopeful speculation? In truth, the mechanism of almost every major step, from chemical precursors up to the first recognizable cells, is the subject of either controversy or complete bewilderment.[15]

Years ago biologist Edwin Conklin summed the matter up quite well: "The probability of life originating from accident is comparable to the probability of the unabridged dictionary resulting from an explosion in a printing shop."[16]

An article in *Scientific American* referred to recent reports in the press suggesting that researchers were on the verge of creating "life in a test tube." The author then stated that *this goal seems more distant than ever*. He quotes Harold P. Klein of Santa Clara University, chairman of a National Academy of Sciences committee that recently reviewed origin-of-life research: "The simplest bacterium is so . . . complicated from the point of view of a chemist that it is almost impossible to imagine how it happened."[17]

The same article points out that the most sophisticated attempt at explaining life origins by naturalistic development has a "hitch": "DNA cannot do its work, including forming more DNA, without the help of catalytic proteins, or enzymes. In short, proteins cannot form without DNA, but neither can DNA form without proteins."[18]

Harvard geneticist Richard Lewontin reconfirms the dilemma faced by those insisting on naturalistic origination for a functioning cell:

> No living molecule is self-replicating. Only whole cells may contain all the necessary machinery for "self"–reproduction. . . . Not only is DNA incapable of making copies of itself, aided or unaided, but it is incapable of "making" anything else. . . . The proteins of the cell are made by other proteins, and without that protein–forming machinery *nothing* can be made. . . . We inherit not only genes made of DNA but **an intricate structure of cellular machinery** [emphasis added].[19]

This is what creationists have been saying all along: that the entire cell mechanism must be in place for the components to work at all! It is becoming increasingly clear that evolution won't work because of insurmountable problems with the origin of life.

Addressing a similar category, let's explore the issue of . . .

1. George Alexander, "How Life on Earth Began," *Reader's Digest*, November 1982, pp. 116–20
2. Patrick Thaddeus, "The Road to Life," *Discover*, March 1988, pp. 69–72
3. Ibid., p. 71
4. Ibid., p. 70
5. Ibid., p. 72
6. David Skjaerlund, "Evolution's Myth About Our Origin," *Destiny*, December 1994, p.22
7. Frederick Hoyle, "Miracle of Biology," *Astronomy*, November 1981, p. 526
8. Skjaerlund, ibid.
9. Ibid., pp. 22,23
10. Ibid., p.23
11. Richard B. Bliss, Gary E. Parker, Duane T. Gish, *Origin of Life*, Creation Life Publishers (San Diego, CA 1990) p. 14
12. Charles B. Thaxton, Walter L. Bradley, Roger L. Olsen, *The Mystery of Life's Origin: Reassessing Current Theories*, Philosophical Library (New York, 1984), pp. 182–187
13. Duane T. Gish, "A Consistent Christian-Scientific View of the Origin of Life," *Creation Research Society Quarterly*, Vol. 15, No. 4, pp. 201–202
14. I. L. Cohen, *Darwin Was Wrong—A Study in Probabilities* (Greenvale, New York: New Research Publications, 1984), p. 205
15. Andrew Scott, "Update on Genesis," *New Scientist*, Vol. 106, May 2, 1985, p. 30
16. Edwin Conklin, *Reader's Digest*, January 1963, p. 92
17. Harold P. Klein, "In The Beginning," *Scientific American*, February 1991, p. 120
18. John Horgan, "In The Beginning," *Scientific American*, February 1991, p. 119
19. Richard Lewontin, "The Dream of the Human Genome," *New York Review of Books*, May 28, 1992, p. 33

Chapter 5

Development in Life Forms

Without question the theory of evolution postulates that man descended from ape, or an ape-like creature. Many naïve onlookers attempt to ignore the implications of this assumption, but evolutionary scholars are less inclined to sidestep the issue. Anthropologist Earnst Hooten was quite forceful in insisting that our heritage included apes:

> If we are descended from apes our remote ancestors ought to look their part. You may not be willing to admit that you resemble an ape; . . . But if that thousandth ancestor's forebearers become progressively more simian as you trace back the genealogical lines you will have to admit that somewhere in your family tree there squats an ape.[1]

How could such a bold assertion be made? If evolution is true, then the assumption is logical. In fact, in that case we are related in some measure to the dinosaurs, the fishes, and the squids! The basic pathway for the supposed progression of life is listed in the chart:

Progression of Life Leading to Man
1. Non-living matter
2. Bacteria, Protozoans
3. Invertebrates

4. Vertebrate fishes
5. Amphibians
6. Reptiles
7. Birds
8. Fur-bearing quadrupeds
9. Apes
10. Man

© 1999 by Steve Miller

The concept is illustrated in the Evolutionary Tree:
The reader should be aware of the fact that this "evolutionary tree" is *make-believe*. Colin Patterson is senior paleontologist at the British Museum of Natural History. His honest appraisal is: "We have access to the tips of a tree; the tree itself is theory and people who pretend to know about the tree and to describe what went on with it, how the branches came off and the twigs came off are, I think, telling stories."[2]

Various scenarios have been introduced to form an evolutionary bridge between gaps separating distinctive life forms. One popular imaginary bridge relates to dinosaurs and feathered flight in birds.[3] The chart is shown along with attendant evolutionary explanations:[4]

Even many evolutionary scientists are unconvinced that dinosaurs sired birds. They argue appropriately that birds and theropod hands differ, manifesting different fingers in differing configurations. They point out that in their geologic timeframe theropods appear too late to give rise to birds, *Protoavis* (a true bird) showing up in the Triassic. And most convincingly, they demonstrate that the complex lungs of birds could not have evolved from theropod lungs. The lungs of birds are extremely complex and are unlike the lungs of any living animal.[5] Other researchers compared the lungs of living birds and crocodiles with evidence from actual dinosaur fossils.

> Crocodiles, like mammals, draw air into their lungs with the help of a diaphragm, a movable tissue that divides the chest cavity from the abdomen. . . . Birds have a different lung system, one that doesn't rely on a diaphragm to alter the pressure in the chest cavity. Instead, muscles connected to the ribs draw air into a network of sacs located in the abdomen—an extremely efficient system for

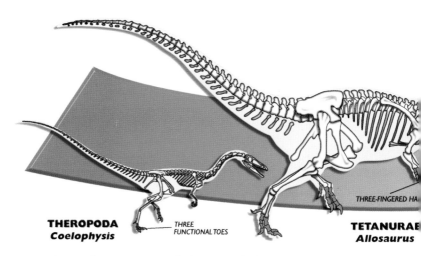

THEROPODA
Coelophysis

THREE
FUNCTIONAL TOES

TETANURAE
Allosaurus

THREE-FINGERED HA

supplying the oxygen needed during flight.

One fossil of [a Chinese dinosaur called *Sinosaurop-teryx*] . . . preserves evidence of internal organs that normally don't show up in dinosaur remains. These soft-tissue impressions in the chest cavity of *Sinosauropteryx* match the shape and placement of the diaphragm of crocodiles, offering further hints that dinosaurs breathed like crocodiles.[6]

The prized trophy that supposedly demonstrates the transition from reptiles to birds is *Archaeopteryx*. How-ever, Duane Gish analyzes the evidence and convinc-ingly demonstrates this creature to be a true bird that can in no way represent a transitional form from reptile to bird.[7] Writing in *Science*, Allan Feduccia came to the same conclusion: "*Archaeopteryx* probably cannot tell us much about the early origins of feathers and flight in true protobirds because *Archaeopteryx* was, in a modern

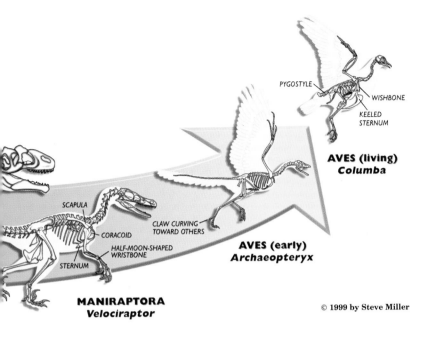

PYGOSTYLE

WISHBONE

KEELED
STERNUM

AVES (living)
Columba

SCAPULA

CLAW CURVING
TOWARD OTHERS

CORACOID

HALF-MOON-SHAPED
WRISTBONE

STERNUM

AVES (early)
Archaeopteryx

MANIRAPTORA
Velociraptor

© 1999 by Steve Miller

sense, a bird."[8]

Not only is the evidence lacking for reptile–to–bird transition, but there is no evidence for such transition anywhere in the fossil record! Steven Stanley conceded this point: "The known fossil record fails to document a single example of phyletic evolution accomplishing a major morphologic transition. . . ."[9] The November 1999 issue of *National Geographic* magazine contained a glowing depiction of *Archaeoraptor lianingensis,* the supposed dinosaur with feathers. However, the January 15, 2000, issue of *Science News* (vol. 157) revealed that ***the central evidence was a fake*** with the feathers of a bird fossil pasted on a dinosaur fossil. Yet, the "morphing game" continues to be played, and a gullible public assumes there is evidence to support the claims.

The most vivid illustration of this sleight-of-hand practice is the emotionally charged subject of supposed

human evolution. According to that view, in the dim distant past, man's ancestors included the fishes; so he is supposed to carry genetic vestiges of "gill slits" in his embryonic development. Actually, what has been interpreted as "gill slits" in the developing human embryo are instead pharyngeal pouches that develop into the lower jaw, parts of the middle ear, and certain glands (see "gill slits" diagram). Roger Lewin quotes Donald

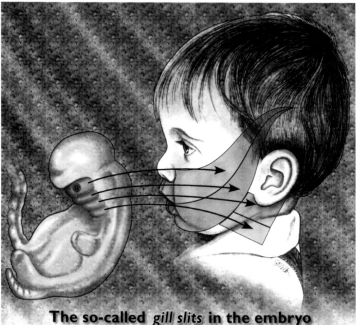

The so-called *gill slits* in the embryo are in reality pharyngeal pouches that develop into the lower jaw, parts of the middle ear and certain glands.

© 1999 by Steve Miller

Johanson (the discoverer of "Lucy," the australopithecine [supposedly] in our ancestry) as noting that "anthropologists who deal with human fossils tend to get very emotionally involved with their bones."[10] Is there any evidence of human evolution? According to the standard evolutionary scenario, man descended from an australopithecine ape, or at least an ape-like creature—common to both man and ape. But the dramatic difference in brain capacity is illustrated in the following diagram:

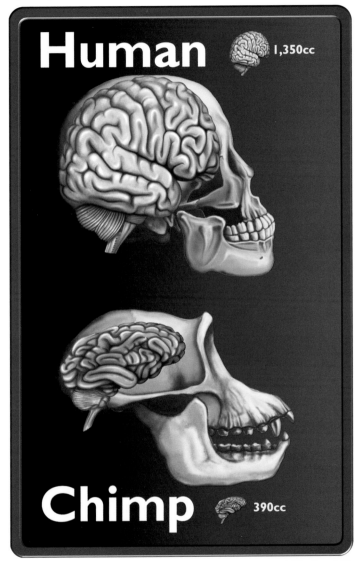

Human 1,350cc

Chimp 390cc

Since the publication of the schematic diagrams shown above, high-tech image studies have actually shrunk the

fossil braincase of prehistoric homi-
nids. Anthropologist Dean Falk of
the State University of New York at
Albany wrote: "The implication of
surprising [smaller] cranial capacity is that something is very wrong
with the published record of early
hominid cranial capacities."[11] In the
literature, reference is made to the
"supposed" upright gait of "Lucy."
But current research has concluded
that "Lucy" was a "tree-climber"
and probably could not walk upright![12]

Evolutionist Charles Oxnard,
professor of anatomy and human
biology at the University of West-
ern Australia, completed the most
sophisticated computer analysis of
australopithecine fossils (of which
"Lucy" is a component) ever under-
taken. He concluded that **they have
nothing to do with the ancestry
of man whatsoever** and are simply
an extinct form of ape.[13] Other recognized anthropologists write that the
hands and feet of *Australopithecus
afarensis* are not at all like human
hands and feet; rather, they have
the long, curved fingers and toes of
typical arboreal primates.[14]

According to popular theory there
should be a smooth line of progression from lower primates (apes) to

**Supposed
Descent of Man
from Primitive
Life Forms**

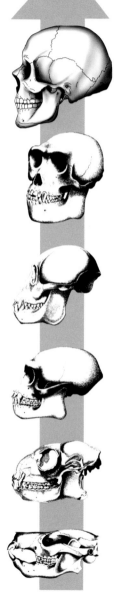

higher primates (man). Most readers would be surprised to learn that the fossils of "alleged" human ancestry are so sparse that all of them would fit inside a single coffin![15]

What is the current status of research about our ancestry among the apes? In December 1996, the late Mary Leakey (one of the world's leading paleoanthropologists) was quoted as saying: "All those trees of life with their branches of our ancestors, that's a lot of nonsense."[16]

Just before his death Louis Leakey published that he had discovered remains of *Homo erectus, Australopithecus,* and *Homo habilis,* in a contemporary Olduvai Gorge bed, with a circular stone "habitation hut" underneath.[17] Modern man is older than his "supposed" ancestors!

Macleans Magazine, science section, reported that Carl Swisher of the Berkeley Geochronology Center made a discovery which places Java Man (*Homo erectus*) "in the era of modern humans . . . and argue[s] against ancestral relationship."[18] *Newsweek* reported that Carl Swisher " . . . published his results and set the world of anthropology on its head."[19]

It, then, is no wonder that Christopher Stringer commented in *Scientific American*: "The study of human origins seems to be a field in which each discovery raises the debate to a more sophisticated level of uncertainty."[20]

These disclosures should give any discerning person reason for pause. And these revelations should encourage agreement with Robert Martin, senior research fellow at the Zoological Society of London. This knowledgeable academician said: "So one is forced to conclude that there is no clearcut scientific picture of human evolution."[21]

The work done by Michael Hammer of the University of Arizona sent shockwaves through the evolutionary community:

We are finding that humans have very, very shallow genetic roots which go back very recently to one ancestor …that indicates that there was an origin in a specific location on the globe and then it spread out from there. …Researchers suggest that virtually all modern men …are closely related genetically and share genes with one male ancestor, dubbed Y-chromosome Adam.[22]

Zoologist Frank Sherwin, writing in *Back to Genesis*, gives us a current update on "human evolution."

We find the track record of human evolution to be dismal:

1. *Ramapithecus*—a pongid or great ape, not a hominid.
2. Piltdown Man—greatest paleontological hoax.
3. Nebraska Man—extinct pig.
4. Cro-Magnon Man—indistinguishable from modern Europeans.
5. *Homo habilis*—wastebasket taxon of fragments.
6. Neanderthals—now recognized to be fully human.
7. *Australopithecus*—ape with no traceable link to man.[23]

A significant article appeared in *Newsweek* entitled "Is Man a Subtle Accident?" The writer appropriately pointed out that

. . . the missing link between man and the apes, whose absence has comforted fundamentalists since the days of Darwin, is merely the most glamorous of a whole hierarchy of phantom creatures. . . . The more scientists have searched for the transitional forms that lie between species, the more they have been frustrated.[24]

Having learned that there is no traceable descent from

ape to man, it seems appropriate to ask the question: **Is it even possible for man to descend from ape, or any other creature?** That is a fair question. Any affirmative answer would require untold mutational changes in the developing organism. But alterations in genetic structure face insurmountable problems. This difficulty was recognized, but ignored, very early in the modern research process. Radiation and mutation specialist James Crow addressed this issue early:

> . . . A mutation is a random change of a highly organized, reasonably smoothly functioning human body. A random change in the highly integrated system of chemical processes which constitute life is certain to impair—just as a random interchange of connections in a television set is not likely to improve the picture.[25]

But modern genetic research has demonstrated that the problem is much more serious than "impairment." Genetics researcher Barney T. Maddox, M.D., has written on the futility of considering such mutational alteration:

> . . . Scientific observation directly contradicts evolutionary theory. The vast, vast majority of genetic mutations are usually lethal, or at least crippling to the organism, drastically damaging survival and function. A few examples in humans include Trisomy 21 (Down's syndrome), polycystic kidney disease, and cystic fibrosis.
>
> . . . The important point is that science has now quantitated that a genetic mutation of as little as 1 billionth (0.0000001 percent) of an animal's genome is relentlessly fatal!
>
> . . . Now the genetic difference between human and his "nearest relative," the chimpanzee, is at least 1.6 percent.

That doesn't sound like much, but calculated out, that is a gap of at least 48 million nucleotide differences that must be bridged by random changes. A random change of only three nucleotides is fatal to an animal (and, of course, the death of a crippled mutant animal ends all possibility of further change).

. . . Obviously there is no way to bridge even small genetic gaps successfully between animal species closely resembling each other.[26]

This observation is verified by Radman and Wagner, writing in *Scientific American:*

Generation after generation, through countless cell divisions, the genetic heritage of living things is scrupulously preserved in DNA. . . . All of life depends on the accurate transmission of information. As genetic messages are passed along through generations of dividing cells, even small mistakes can be life-threatening.[27]

Creationists certainly recognize variations within genetic boundaries. These changes are horizontal in effect and produce no new "kind." This is called *micro*evolution. *Macro*evolution refers to major evolutionary changes over time *beyond genetic boundaries.*

In 1980 the University of Chicago hosted a conference of the world's leading evolutionary theorists. The conference was entitled "Macroevolution," and their task was

to consider the mechanisms that underlie the origin of species. The central question of the Chicago conference was whether the mechanisms underlying *micro*evolution can be extrapolated to explain the phenomena of *macro*evolution . . . the answer can be given as a clear, **No.**[28]

Wolfgang Smith held faculty positions at Oregon State, MIT, and UCLA. His considered opinion is expressed rather forcefully: "[Macroevolution] is **totally bereft of scientific sanction**. . . . [T]here exists to this day **not a shred of bona fide scientific evidence** in support of the thesis that macroevolutionary transformations ever occurred [emphasis added]."[29]

Darwin lamented: "Geology assuredly does not reveal any such finely graduated organic chain; and this, perhaps, is the most obvious and gravest objection which can be urged against my theory [of evolution]."[30]

There is no scientific data in the fossil record to demonstrate that one living system developed into another; and there are no laboratory experiments indicating that the feat would **even be possible.** What we actually find is a condition termed . . .

---

1. Earnst A. Hooten, *Up From the Ape* (New York: MacMillan) p. 289
2. Colin Patterson, "Cladistics," Interview of British Broadcasting Corporation television program on March 4, 1982; producer, Brian Leek; Interviewer, Peter Franz
3. Kevin Padian and Luis M. Chiappe, "The Origin of Birds and Their Flight," *Scientific American*, February 1998, pp. 38–47
4. Compare ibid., pp. 40,41
5. Ibid., p. 43
6. R. Monastersky, "Biologists Peck at Bird–Dinosaur Link," *Science News*, Vol. 152, November 15, 1997, pp. 310–11
7. Duane Gish, *Evolution: The Fossils Still Say NO!* (El Cajon, CA: Institute For Creation Research, 1995) pp. 129–45
8. Allan Feduccia, *Science* 259:790–793 (1993)
9. Steven M. Stanley, *Macroevolution: Pattern and Process* (San Francisco: W. M. Freeman and Company, 1979), p. 39
10. Roger Lewin, *Bones of Contention* (New York: Simon and Schuster, 1987)
11. B. Bower quoting Dean Falk, "High-tech Images Shrink Fossil Braincase," *Science News*, Vol. 153, June 13, 1998, p. 374
12. William L. Jungers, "Lucy's Limbs: Skeletal Allometry and Locomotion in *Australopithicus Afarensis*," *Nature*, Vol. 24, June 1982, pp. 676–78

13. Charles Oxnard, *The Order of Man* (Yale University Press, 1984)
14. Stern and Susman, *American Journal of Physical Anthropology* 60:279–313 (1983)
15. Lyall Watson, "The Water People," *Science Digest*, Vol. 90, May 1982, p. 44
16. Frank Sherwin, " 'Human Evolution' An Update," *Back to Genesis*, (El Cajon, CA: Institute for Creation Research, September 1997), p. a
17. Louis S. B. Leakey, "New Finds at Olduvai Gorge," *Nature*, Vol. 189 (February 25, 1961), p. 649
18. *Macleans Magazine*, science section, December 23, 1996
19. *Newsweek*, December 23, 1996
20. Christopher B. Stringer, "The Legacy of Homo Sapiens," *Scientific American*, Vol. 268, May 1993, p. 138
21. Robert Martin, "Man Is Not an Onion," *New Scientist*, Vol. 75, No. 1063, August 4, 1977, p. 285
22. *U.S. News & World Report*, December 4, 1995
23. Frank Sherwin, " 'Human Evolution' Update," *Back to Genesis*, (El Cajon, CA: Institute for Creation Research, September 1997), p. b
24. "Is Man a Subtle Accident?" *Newsweek*, November 3, 1980
25. James F. Crow, "Genetic Effects of Radiation," *Bulletin of the Atomic Scientists*, Vol. 14 (1958), pp. 19–20
26. Barney T. Maddox, *Human Genome Project: Quantitative Disproof of Evolution* (Cleburne, TX: Self-published, 1992) pp. 1–3
27. Miroslav Radman and Robert Wagner, "The High Fidelity of DNA Duplication," *Scientific American*, Vol. 259, No. 2, August 1988, p. 24
28. Lewin, *Science* Vol. 210, pp. 883–87
29. Wolfgang Smith, *Teilhardism and the New Religion* (Tan Books 1988), pp. 5–6
30. Charles Darwin, *The Origin of Species by Means of Natural Selection*, first edition reprint (New York: Avenel Books, 1979), p. 292

Chapter 6

Stasis

Stasis simply means "to remain the same." The evolutionist looks at the fossil record as representing hundreds of millions of years (the subject of long geologic ages is addressed in another section of this work). But he is puzzled to find stasis in every fossil bed.

"As is now well known, most fossil species appear instantaneously in the fossil record, persist for some millions of years virtually unchanged, only to disappear abruptly...."[1]

Stephen J. Gould, evolution's leading proponent, readily admits that stasis is a recognized principle in fossil discovery: "Stasis, as palpable and observable in virtually all cases...."[2] "Stasis is now generally recognized as an intriguing puzzle by evolutionists. No definite solution is in sight."[3]

Other modern evolutionary scientists readily agree: "Eldredge and Gould, by contrast, decided to take the record at face value. On this view, there is little evidence of modification between species, or of forms intermediate between species, because neither generally occurred."[4]

The earliest fossils deposited were bacteria-like organisms. William Schopf, paleontologist at the University of California at Los Angeles, was struck by the apparent similarities between some one billion–year–old fossils (by evolutionary age assignment) of blue-green bacteria and their modern microbial counterparts. "They surprisingly looked exactly like modern species."[5]

The general public has been led to believe that bacteria have evolved resistance to antibiotics during our lifetime. An actual case in point dispels this notion. In 1849 John Franklin and his crew were shipwrecked in the Arctic during an expedition. In the course of time all the men died and were buried in the frozen tundra by their comrades (except for the final man whose body was left exposed). In 1989 the University of Saskatchewan sent an expeditionary group to recover the frozen bodies. During autopsy bacteria were found in the intestines. These bacteria, frozen for almost a century and a half, were cultured and exposed to antibiotics. They were found to be resistant to both natural and synthetic antibiotics![6] The resistance is genetic; it has not developed by mutations.

Fruit flies represent an organism whose mutants have probably been studied more than any other. Radiation can alter their normal appearance in many respects, but after radiation they return to normal characteristics when released among original stock. "The fruit-fly (*Drosophila melanogaster*), the favorite pet insect of the geneticists, whose geographical, biotopical, urban, and rural genotypes are now known inside out, seems not to have changed since the remotest times."[7]

Of even greater interest are the **living fossils,** creatures that are alive today—yet have identical counterparts deep in the fossil record.

Both blue-green algae and bacteria fossils dating back 3.4 billion years [by evolutionary geologic age assignments] have been found in rocks from South Africa. . . . Even more intriguing, the . . . algae turned out to be almost identical to modern . . . algae at the family and possibly even at the generic level.[8]

Nearly all living phyla of marine invertebrates that have reasonably good fossil records have first occurrences either in the late Precambrian or early to middle Cambrian. At the class level there are 27 paleontologically important living groups and all have documented occurrences which are Silurian or older.[9]

The order of life and the persistence of nearly all basic anatomical designs throughout the entire geological history of multicellular animals record the intricacy and resistance to change of complex development programs.[10]

Why have these creatures not changed during the time they have inhabited this planet? Or, if there has been any change at all, why is it limited to mere ecological adaptation? The limits of this adaptation (or microevolution) is within the genetic confines of each kind. "Microevolution does not lead beyond the confines of the species, and the typical products of microevolution, the geographic races, are not incipient species. There is no such category as incipient species."[11] (Incipient: the early, initial stages of something new.) "Microevolution . . . leads to diversification strictly within the species."[12]

There is a profound and fundamental reason for the limits of variation and adaptation, which are confined strictly within the species. The simple reason is that the DNA faithfully replicates its information and protects its own integrity. Of most profound impact in organic chemistry was the discovery that enzymes within the cell **actually repair any errors or damage in the DNA!** The profound nature of this discovery was emphasized by professor D. H. R. Barton (Nobel Prize for chemistry):

"The genome is reproduced very faithfully and there are enzymes which repair the DNA, where errors have been made or when the DNA is damaged."[13]

Evolution won't work, because stasis is maintained within living systems. This leads us to examination of...

1. Tom Kemp, "A Fresh Look at the Fossil Record," *New Scientist*, Vol. 108, December 5, 1985, p. 67

2. Stephen J. Gould and Niles Eldredge, "Punctuated Equilibrium Comes to Age," *Nature*, Vol. 366, November 18, 1993, p. 223

3. Stephen J. Gould, "Opus 200," *Natural History*, August 1991, p. 16

4. Peter J. Smith, "Evolution's Most Worrisome Questions," *New Scientist*, Vol. 116, November 19, 1987, p. 59

5. J. William Schopf, quoted by Elizabeth Pennisi, "Static Evolution," *Science News*, March 12, 1994, p. 168

6. Mark Eastman, M.D., "From Goo to the Zoo to You," *Creation vs. Evolution*, Chuck Missler Audio Series

7. Pierre P. Grasse, *Evolution of Living Organisms* (New York: Academic Press, 1977), p. 130

8. "Ancient Algae Fossil Most Complex Yet," *Science News*, Vol. 108, September 20, 1975, p. 181. See also "Static Evolution," *Science News*, Vol. 145, March 12, 1994, p. 168–69.

9. David M. Raup, "On the Early Origins of Major Biologic Groups," *Paleobiology*, Vol. 9, No. 2 (1983), p. 107

10. Stephen J. Gould, "Through a Lens, Darkly," *Natural History*, September 1989, p. 24

11. Richard B. Goldschmidt, *The Material Basis of Evolution* (Patterson, New Jersey: Pageant Books, 1960), p. 396

12. Ibid., p. 183

13. Henry Margenau and Roy Abraham Varghese, *Cosmos, Bios, Theos* (La Salle, IL: Open Court, 1992), p. 146

Chapter 7

The Geologic Column, Its Fossils and Artifacts

The geologic column is the "Bible" of evolutionary dogma. Sir Charles Lyell is credited with its formulation, at least in modern times. But its roots reach back to the ancient beliefs of pagan philosophers.[1] It is a "supposed" column in which fossils of "early" life forms should be buried near the bottom, "intermediate" forms should be enclosed in progressive order, and "recent" systems should be found in higher strata. It is envisioned to represent the early formation of Planet Earth, subsequent development of life from nonliving chemicals, and the progression of living systems leading to man.

This column is fundamental to all evolutionary interpretations, yet **it is not found intact anywhere on earth—except in the mind of the evolutionist!** Evolutionist Derek Ager chided his companions for assuming otherwise. "We are only kidding ourselves if we think that we have anything like a complete succession for any part of the stratigraphical column in any one place."[2]

It is actually a theory that is *forcefully imposed* upon the evidence, without justification. Geologist John Woodmorappe said the column was essentially nonexistent and that it was a fantastic and imaginative contrivance.

Since only a small percentage of the earth's surface

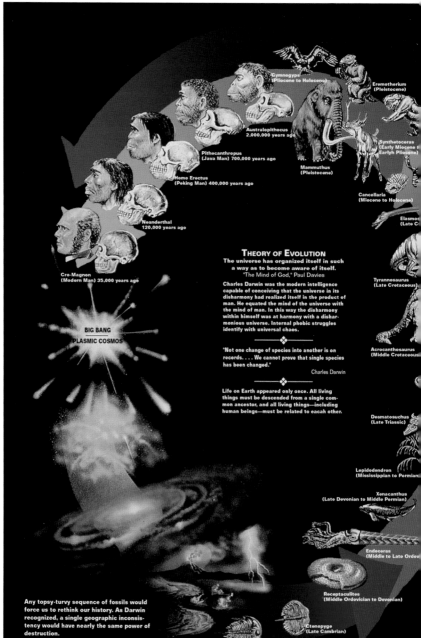

Gymnogyps
(Pliocene to Holocene)

Eremotherium
(Pleistocene)

Australopithecus
2,000,000 years ago

Synthetoceras
(Early Miocene t
Earlyh Pliocene)

Pithecanthropus
(Java Man) 700,000 years ago

Mammuthus
(Pleistocene)

Home Erectus
(Peking Man) 400,000 years ago

Cancellaria
(Miocene to Holocene)

Neanderthal
120,000 years ago

Elasmo
(Late C

Cro-Magnon
(Modern Man) 35,000 years ago

Tyrannosaurus
(Late Cretaceous)

THEORY OF EVOLUTION
The universe has organized itself in such
a way as to become aware of itself.
"The Mind of God," Paul Davies

Charles Darwin was the modern intelligence
capable of conceiving that the universe in its
disharmony had realized itself in the product of
man. He equated the mind of the universe with
the mind of man. In this way the disharmony
within himself was at harmony with a dishar-
monious universe. Internal phobic struggles
identify with universal chaos.

BIG BANG
PLASMIC COSMOS

"Not one change of species into another is on
records. . . . We cannot prove that single species
has been changed."

Charles Darwin

Acrocanthosaurus
(Middle Cretaceous)

Life on Earth appeared only once. All living
things must be descended from a single common ancestor, and all living things—including
human beings—must be related to eacah other.

Desmatosuchus
(Late Triassic)

Lepidodendron
(Mississippian to Permian)

Xenacanthus
(Late Devonian to Middle Permian)

Endoceras
(Middle to Late Ordovi

Receptaculites
(Middle Ordovician to Devonian)

Any topsy-turvy sequence of fossils would
force us to rethink our history. As Darwin
recognized, a single geographic inconsistency would have nearly the same power of
destruction.

The New Evolutionary Timetable, 1981, p. 171
Stephen M. Stanley, Johns Hopkins University

Ctenopyge
(Late Cambrian)

Olenellus
(Early Cambrian)

Time Period
MID-PLEISTOCENE
LOWER PLEISTOCENE
PLIOCENE
MIOCENE/ OLIGOCENE
EOCENE
PALEOCENE
CRETACEOUS
JURASSIC/ TRIASSIC
PERMIAN
PENNSYLVANIAN
MISSISSIPPIAN/ DEVONIAN
SILURIAN/ ORDOVICIAN
CAMBRIAN

Supposed Evolutionary Progression in the Geologic Column

obeys even a significant portion of the geologic column, it becomes an overall exercise of gargantuan special pleading and imagination for the evolutionary-uniformitarian paradigm to maintain that there ever *were* geologic periods. The claim of their having taken place to form a continuum of rock/life/time . . . over the earth is therefore a fantastic and imaginative contrivance.[3]

Noted botanist and evolutionist N. Heribert Nilsson exposed the deficiencies as being real.

My attempts to demonstrate evolution by an experiment carried on for more than forty years have completely failed. . . . It may be firmly maintained that it is not even possible to make a caricature of an evolution out of paleobiological facts. The fossil material is now so complete... and the lack of transitional series cannot be explained as being due to the scarcity of material. The deficiencies are real, they will never be filled.[4]

And the problem is even worse than is admitted. Paleontologist H. S. Ladd of the University of California at Berkeley speaks about the missing chain.

> Most paleontologists today give little thought to the fossiliferous rocks older than the Cambrian, thus ignoring the most important missing link of all. Indeed the missing pre-Cambrian record cannot properly be described as a link, for it is in reality about nine-tenths of the chain of life: the first nine-tenths.[5]

In designing the geologic column, naturalists *assumed evolution to be true*—then went about to interpret whatever was found in the rocks *as if evolution were factual*. The sedimentary layers are interpreted as encasing a progressive sequence of fossilized life forms. This is supposed to hold true, even if no more than a single fossil group is present, or even if the order of progression is inverted![6]

Dating the fossils by the rocks and the rocks by the fossils is self-serving circular reasoning. Some fair-minded evolutionists are making admissions on this issue. "The intelligent layman has long suspected circular reasoning in the use of rocks to date fossils and fossils to date rocks. The geologist has never bothered to think of a good reply, feeling the explanations are not worth the trouble as long as the work brings results."[7]

We have already seen that the fossils appear suddenly in the sedimentary layers. It must also be admitted that the same record requires extensive catastrophic activity. "The geologic record does seem to require catastrophes."[8]

The fossil record actually demonstrates special creation. An esteemed professor of botany at Cambridge University agrees. ". . . I still think that to the unprejudiced, the fossil record of plants is in favor of special creation."[9]

There is an added degree to which the fossil record demonstrates special creation. The research at the Creation Evidence Museum in Glen Rose, Texas, has presented for public scrutiny an impressive collection of artifacts. These artifacts were discovered scattered throughout much of the geologic column. Their importance can be realized by glancing at this quote by Richard Dawkins, one of evolution's most brilliant thinkers.

> We should be very surprised . . . to find fossil humans appearing in the record before mammals are supposed to have evolved! If a single, well-verified mammal skull were to turn up in 500 million–year–old rocks, our whole modern theory of evolution would be utterly destroyed.[10]

Steven Stanley verified the same principle.

> There is an infinite variety of ways in which, since 1859, the general concept of evolution might have been demolished. Consider the fossil record—a little known resource in Darwin's day. The unequivocal discovery of a fossil population of horses in pre-Cambrian rocks would disprove evolution. More generally, any topsy-turvy sequence of fossils would force us to rethink our theory, yet not a single one has come to light. As Darwin recognized, a single geographic inconsistency would have nearly the same power of destruction.[11]

The following display of artifacts cannot be easily dismissed.

In 1983 D. H. Milne and S. Schafersman wrote in the *Journal of Geological Education* about the reports of finding human prints and dinosaur prints in the same rock stratum. "Such an occurrence would seriously disrupt conventional interpretations of the biological and geological history and would support the doctrines of creationism and catastrophism."[12]

Entire books have been written supporting the concept that man-made artifacts have been found scattered

The author poses beside a human footprint in Permian rock. In 1987 Jerry MacDonald discovered a wide variety of beautifully preserved fossil footprints in the Robledos Mountains of New Mexico. Rumors were heard about "out of place" fossils, but the site remains top secret. Finally, a tantalizing article appeared in the July 1992 *Smithsonian* magazine. The article acknowledged "what paleontologists like to call 'problematics.'" It described what appeared to be large mammal and bird tracks that "evolved long after the Permian period, yet these tracks are clearly Permian." With a little detective work and some luck we located the area and even more obvious *"problematica"*—a human footprint in Permian rock!

Max Han was fishing with his wife near London, Texas, when he found a rock with wood protruding from it. When the rock was cracked open, this octagonally shaped iron hammer was exposed. The wood handle is partially coalified with quartz and calcite crystalline inclusions. Tests performed at Battelle Laboratory document the hammer's unusual metallurgy: 96.6% iron; 2.6% chlorine; and 0.74% sulfur (no carbon). Density tests indicate forging of exceptional quality. A unique coating of FeO, which does not readily form under present atmospheric conditions, appears to inhibit rusting. The enclosing rock contains Lower Cretaceous

fossils. It is a concretionary sandstone nodule from the nearby cliff which is made up of such nodules. This cliff is part of the Lower Cretaceous Edwards Plateau which evolutionists tell us was formed 140 million years ago, when dinosaurs roamed the earth. Of course, the coexistence of humans and dinosaurs would destroy evolutionary theory, so maybe the hammer was made by dinosaurs. Do you really think so?

The *Burdick Print* is in Cretaceous limestone, found near Glen Rose, Texas (famous for its dinosaur tracks). Evolutionary theory claims that humans were separated from these dino-

saurs by over 100 million years, and therefore evolutionsts assume the tracks were carved.

This assumption has been disproved by cross-sectioning. Carving would randomly cut across the internal rock structures. However, if those structures follow the contours of the impression, the carving theory would be falsified. Internal structures dramatically conform to the shape of both the *heel* impression (top left) and the *great toe* impression (below right), demonstrating that this is an original impression in limestone well known for dinosaur prints.

Jerry Simons (bottom right) used junior high students to make tracks in wet concrete. They demonstrated that a wide variety of shapes can be produced by normal-looking feet. Standing prints leave a slanted row of rounded dots at the end of the "hourglass" shaped prints. Running prints have a different set of peculiar characteristics: pronated toes, raised centers, wide anteriors, narrow posteriors. The bottom left picture shows one running track coming forward and another going away. Similarity to the *Burdick Track* is striking.

This fossil footprint (+3) is one of fourteen that make up the Taylor Trail, a sequence of very human-like tracks found with at least 134 dinosaur tracks in the bed of the Palux River. The picture on the top shows the track when first excavated, about 1972.

Sixteen years later erosion had removed a thin veneer of rock and was revealed that the track was actually within a dinosaur track that was not visible initially. The dinosaur track is flush with the surface for the most part and slightly redder in color, indicating infill material. When viewed through the water, only the dinosaur track is obvious (bottom right). However, when the water goes down, the human-shaped depression can still be seen (bottom left).

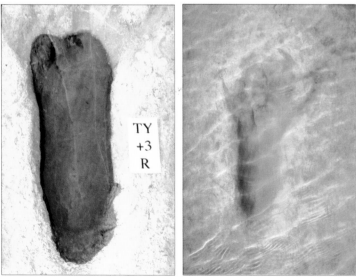

Stan Taylor (left) began his excavation of the Taylor Trail in 1969 and continued working through 1972. Initially, only two tracks could be seen in the Paluxy River bed. By following the trail back under the river bank, seven more very human-like tracks were exposed. The process involved removing tons of limestone overburden, effectively eliminating the possibility that the tracks might be carved.

Subsequent excavation has extended the trail to a total of fourteen tracks in a consistent left-right pattern. The entire sequence can be seen through the water in this 1994 photograph (top right), even though a thin layer of mud obscures the details. A trail of three-toed dinosaur tracks can be seen crossing at an angle of approximately 30 degrees.

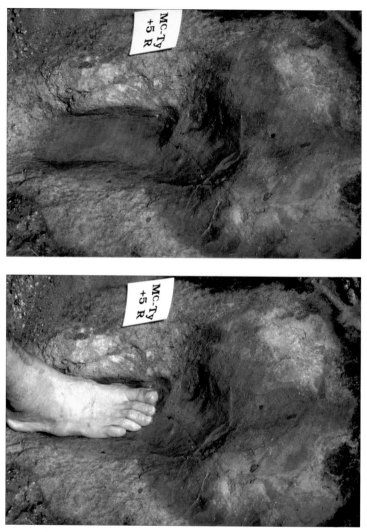

These three views of the same fossil footprints appear in the bed of the Paluxy River, famous for its dinosaur tracks. Dinosaur Valley State Park is near by. Here, the 11.5" human-like footprint is superimposed on the heel of a 25" dinosaur track. This right footprint (+5) is followed by a left (+6) which is also 11.5" in length. The right-left pattern is consistent throughout the entire sequence of fourteen 11.5" footprints known as Taylor Trail.

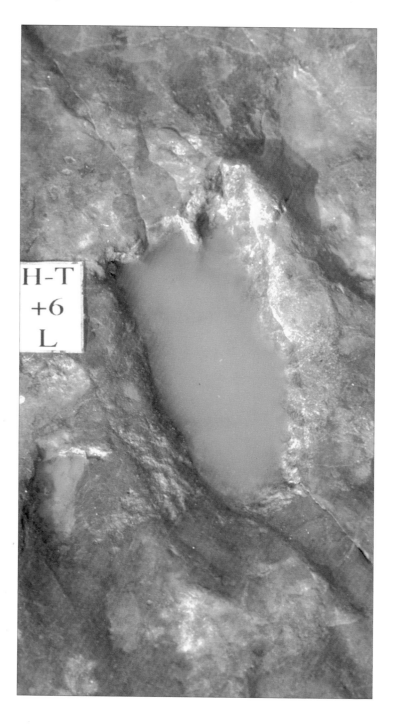

The 1988 photograph to the left shows a very human-like fossil footprint in the bed of the Paluxy River near Glen Rose, Texas. This left footprint is in a sequence of fourteen that are left-right consistent and consistently about 11.5" in length. The tracks were excavated from beneath six feet of alternating layers of clay and limestone. The surrounding "mud push up" helps demonstrate authenticity.

By 1992 erosion revealed (top right) that this footprint was directly beside one of the 134 dinosaur prints on the same platform. The entire trail of human-like tracks is among, within, across and, in this case, *beside* 25" dinosaur tracks.

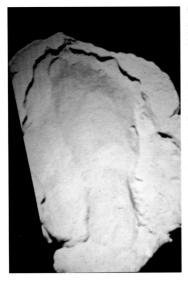

The cast (left) of a fossil footprint was made by Stan Taylor in 1970. The print (+1) is one in 14-track Taylor Trail.

The lower left picture of the same print, taken in 1988, shows the effect of 18 years of erosion. A chunk came out of the left side, but the same general shape can be seen.

On August 12, 1989, geologist Don Patton spoke at a creation conference in Dayton, Tennessee. He presented evidence that all the data relating to the Taylor Trail was best explained by a combination of human and dinosaur tracks. He featured this track and -3B. After saboteurs gouged out the details with an iron bar, it was observed looking like the picture bottom right.

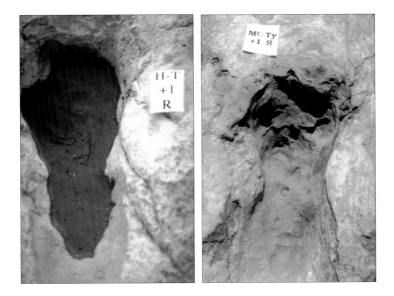

The fossil footprint seen in these pictures is called the *Ryals Track,* named for Jim Ryals, who removed a beautiful left footprint from the Paluxy River bed, back in the '30s. The resulting hole in the Cretaceous limestone can be seen directly ahead of this right footprint. The track Ryals removed was on display for years in the courtyard of Dr. Cook's medical clinic in Cleburne, Texas.

The toes of this track extend back under an overhang formed when the foot was pulled out of the calcareous "mud." The same feature can be seen in some of the hundreds of dinosaur tracks found in the same layer. When the individual stepped forward the toes drug, leaving impressions in the now hard limestone.

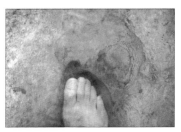

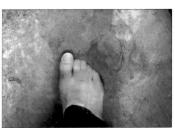

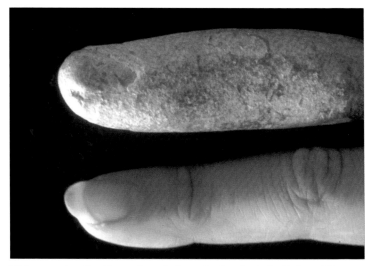

This amazing fossil was found along the bank of the Paluxy River a number of years ago. It has recently been sectioned to reveal the typical porous bone structure expected in a human finger. Examinations by means of a CT scan and MRI allowed Dr. Dale Peterson, M.D. (lower left) to identify joints and to trace tendons throughout the length of the fossil.

Some had argued that it could not be a fossilized finger since pressuring from overlying layers compresses and flattens. This is usually true, but not in the Glen Rose formation. Several locations reveal thousands of fossilized worms (lower right) that are perfectly three dimensional. If anything should be flattened it would be worms, but they are not. Obviously, very rapid lithification is required in order to preserve such astonishing detail.

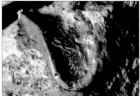

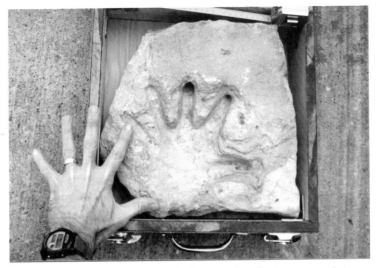

This photo shows a human handprint found in Cretaceous rock in the same layer with the Glen Rose dinosaur footprints. The fossil handprint is so specific that it displays impressions of the thumbnail, impressions of the tissue webbing between the thumb and index finger, and the impression left by penetration of the middle finger into the mud.

This 9 3/4-inch human footprint was excavated inside a dinosaur footprint on July 3, 1997, by the Creation Evidence Museum team. The second photo shows paleontologist Floyd Jones of Houston, Texas, verifying the authenticity and the identification of the two fossil footprints.

Tombs in the deserts of Peru often preserve amazing artifacts which are very old, including the beautiful, intricate textiles of the Nasca culture (ca. A.D. 700). These textiles depict living dinosaurs, as do their ceremonial burial stones and pottery, indicating that these awesome creatures were still alive at the time and ancient Peruvians saw them.

INCA BURIAL STONES

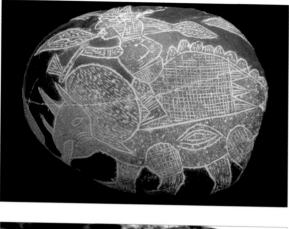

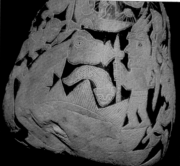

Dr. Javier Cabrera M.D. (lower left with geologist Don Patton) was professor of medicine and head of his department at the University of Lima. He has retired from that position and is presently the cultural anthropologist for Ica, Peru. In the early 1930s, his father found many of these ceremonial burial stones in the area's numerous Inca tombs. Dr. Cabrera has continued his father's research and has collected over 1,100 of them. Approximately one-third depict the pornographic culture of the Incas, graphically portrayed in the artifacts of that period (ca. A.D. 500–1500). Some picture their idolatry (lower right), others represent amazing accomplishments, such as successful brain surgery (center left) confirmed by scarred skulls which demonstrate healed recovery.

Almost one-third of the stones depict scientific types of dinosaurs, like those seen below, as well as Triceratops, Stegosaurus,and pterosaurs. Several Diplodocus-like dinosaurs have what appear to be dermal frills. Confirmation of these features has been reported only recently (*Geology,* 12/92, vol. 20, no. 12, p. 1068–70).

The Indian chronicler, Juan de Santa Cruz Pachachuti Llamgui wrote that at the time of the Inca many carved stones were found in the kingdom of Chinca, in Chinchayunga, which were called *Manco.* The reference to "Chinchayunga" was the low country of the central coast of Peru, where Ica is located today. *Manco* is believed to be a corruption of the Aymara word *malku,* which means "chieftain" or "lord of vassals." It is noted that some of these stones were taken back to Spain. The chronicler of the Incas wrote in about 1570.

On October 3, 1993, the *OJO, Lima Domingo,* a major newspaper in Lima, Peru, described a Spanish priest traveling in the area of Ica in 1525 inquiring about the unusual engraved stones with strange animals on them.

All of this is very interesting since "modern" man's conception of dinosaurs did not begin until the 1800s when the word "dinosaur" was coined (1841). These stones do not depict skeletons, but live, active dinosaurs, most of whom are seen interacting with man. The obvious implication is that ancient Peruvians saw and lived with dinosaurs. Associate Dennis Swift led our expeditions into this area.

THE LIMES

Everyone has heard, "We know for certain it takes millions and millions of years for fossils to petrify." It's so obvious that no proof is necessary, and of course no witnesses verify. The claim is just repeated over and over. So we hear, "Everybody knows that."

Really? How old do you think this boot could be? Millions of years old? Do you really think so? The rubber-soled boot with petrified cowboy leg, bones and all, was found about 1980 in a dry creek bed near the West Texas town of Iraan by Mr. Jerry Stone, an employee of Corvette oil company.

The boot was hand made by the M. L. Leddy boot company of San Angelo, Texas, which began manufacturing boots in 1936. Gayland Leddy, nephew of the founder, grew up in the boot business and now manages Boot Town in Garland, Texas. He recognized the "number 10 stitch pattern" used by his uncle's company where he worked for many years. Mr. Leddy believes the boot was made in the early 1950s.

NE COWBOY

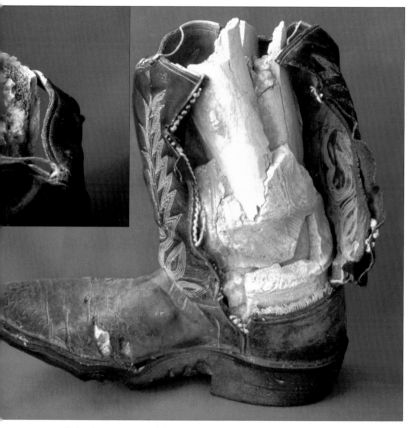

Only the contents of the boot are fossilized, not the boot itself, demonstrating that some materials fossilize more readily than others. The bones of the partial leg and foot within the boot were revealed by an elaborate set of CT scans performed at Harris Methodist Hospital in Ft. Worth, Texas, on July 24, 1997. The radiologic technician was Evelyn Americus, AART. A complete set of these scans remains with the boot at the Creation Evidence Museum in Glen Rose, Texas.

The fact that some materials can fossilize rapidly under certain circumstances is well known by experts in the field and is not really a scientific issue. However, the general public has been misled in order to facilitate the impression of great ages. The dramatic example of the "Limestone Cowboy" immediately communicates the truth of the matter. Fossilization proves nothing about long periods of time.

Time Period	Human Artifacts in the Geological Column
MID-PLEISTOCENE	SKULL .... Olmo, Italy SKELETON ....Clichy, France SKELETON ....Gally Hill, England
LOWER PLEISTOCENE	PELVIS .... Natchez, North America JAW ....Abbeville, France UPPER ARMBONE .... Kanapol, Africa
PLIOCENE	SKULL........................ Calaveras, California SKULL ....Castenolo, Italy SKULL .... Table Mt., California FOOTPRINTS ....Lactolil, Africa SANDAL PRINTS .... Carson City, Nevada
MIOCENE/ OLIGOCENE	SKULL ....Stanford, California JAW ....Tuscany, Italy SHOE PRINT .... Gobi Desert, Asia
EOCENE	SKULL...Germany TOOTH.................... Bear Creek, Montana
PALEOCENE	CAST IRON CUBE .... Wolfberg, Austria
CRETACEOUS	SKELETONS (2) .... La Sal, Utah SKULL ....Gilman, Colorado FOOTPRINTS & FINGER ......Glen Rose, Texas CAST METAL NODULES ....France METAL HAMMER....................London, Texas
JURASSIC/TRIASSIC	LEG & FOOT BONES .... Spring Valley, Nev. FOOTPRINT...................Parkersburg, W. Vir.
PERMIAN	FOOTPRINTS ....Secora, New Mexico FOOTPRINTS ....St. Louis, Missouri HANDPRINTS..........Robledos Mtns., N. Mex.
PENNSYLVANIAN	FOOTPRINTS .... Berea, Kentucky IRON POT....................................Oklahoma TOOLS.................. Abden-Provence, France GOLD CHAIN ....Illinois
MISSISSIPPIAN/DEVONIAN	FOOTPRINTS ....Missouri PRECISION PATTERN ....Pittsburgh, Pa.
SILURIAN/ORDOVICIAN	SKELETON .... Franklin County, Missouri SANDAL PRINT........Lake Windermere, Eng.
CAMBRIAN	SANDAL & FOOTPRINT .... Antelope Spgs, Ut. IRON BANDS .... Lochmaree, Scotland

throughout the geologic column. The reader is referred to *Ancient Man: A Handbook of Puzzling Artifacts* by William R. Corliss[13] and *Forbidden Archaeology* by Michael A. Cremo and Richard L. Thompson.[14] The following chart demonstrates how every era, from the earliest to the most recent, encloses evidence and artifacts associated with man.

Actually, the entire geologic column is of recent origin and is best explained by the events of a worldwide flood, the flood of Noah's day. If there is evidence that man has existed from the earliest sedimentary layers of the geologic column then, in the words of Richard Dawkins, the whole modern theory of evolution has been academically destroyed. Additionally, such evidence is undeniable support for special creation.

Evolution won't work, because the very record that is designed to display its progression favors special creation! Let's now turn our attention to . . .

1. Henry M. Morris and John D. Morris, "Science and Creation," *The Modern Creation Trilogy* (Green Forest, AR: Master Books, 1997), p. 20

2. Derek V. Ager, *The Nature of the Stratigraphical Record* (New York: John Wiley & Sons, 1981), p. 32

3. John Woodmorappe, "The Essential Non-Existence of the Evolutionary Uniformitarian Geologic Column: A Quantitative Assessment," *Creation Research Society Quarterly*, Vol, 18, No. 1, (Terre Haute, Indiana, June 1981), pp. 46–71

4. N. Heribert Nilsson, as quoted in Arthur C. Custance, *The Earth Before Man*, Part II, Doorway Paper, No. 20 (Ontario, Canada: Doorway Publications), p. 51

5. H. S. Ladd, *Memoir 67*, Vol. II (Geological Society of America, 1957), p. 7

6. Alan H. Cutler and Karl W. Plessa, "Fossils Out of Sequence: Computer Simulations and Strategies for Dealing with Stratigraphic Disorder, " *Palaios*, Vol. 5, June 1990, p. 227

7. J. E. O'Rourke, "Pragmatism Versus Materialism in Stratigraphy," *American Journal of Science*, Vol. 276, No. 1, January 1976, p. 48

8. Stephen J. Gould, a review of "Darwin's 'Big Book'." *Science,* May

23, 1975, pp. 824–26

9. Edred J. H. Corner, *Evolution in Contemporary Botanical Thought* (Chicago: Quadrangle Books, 1961), p. 97

10. Richard Dawkins, *The Blind Watchmaker* (New York: W. W. Norton, 1987), p. 255

11. Steven M. Stanley, *The New Evolutionary Timetable: Fossils, Genes and the Origin of Species* (Basic Books, 1981), p. 171

12. D. H. Milne and S. Schafersman, *Journal of Geological Education* 1983, p. 111

13. William R. Corliss, *Ancient Man: A Handbook of Puzzling Artifacts* (Glen Arm, MD: The Sourcebook Project, 1978)

14. Michael A. Cremo and Richard L. Thompson, *Forbidden Archaeology* (Los Angeles: Bhaktivedanta Book Publishing, 1996)

Chapter 8

The Time Factor

In order for evolution to have a whisper of a chance to work, vast ages have been written into its fabric. According to the story, extensive time would be required for stars to form after a cosmic explosion from a Big Bang. Massive amounts of time would be required for those stars to "cook" the heavier elements, then release them throughout the universe in numerous supernova explosions. Afterward, expanded periods would be required for the space debris to form planets. Additional ages would be required for nonliving chemicals to form organic compounds, then for life to evolve and develop to our present state of existence.

These vast ages are simply "assumed" by the evolutionary community. Yet they remain illusive. Each attempt to verify **great universal age** is met with new data conflicting earlier assertions. It must be continually re-examined.

> The conundrum continues. Yet another set of observations indicates that the universe—as described by a popular cosmological model—appears to be younger than its oldest stars. . . . Astronomers have come to a crossroads. They must either embrace a more complex cosmological model or re-examine how they estimate stellar ages."[1]

A recent origin of the universe is indicated by observable

data, such as the physics of rotating galaxies.

[These rotating galaxies] must be of recent origin or
they would have long ago disintegrated the groupings by
their tremendous velocities exceeding the escape speeds
of the clusters.[2]

We know of no process that can maintain a spiral arm for
more than two galactic revolutions.[3]

If this theory is true, the universe is young, since it has
so many rapidly revolving spirals.[4]

Barry Setterfield and D. Russell Humphreys have introduced viable models of universal history that deal with
light arriving from the distant stars. Both models intro-
duce physical data demonstrating a young universe.[5, 6] In
some cosmological models the velocity of light was much
faster in the past, and has since slowed to its present speed
of 186,282.0244866 miles per second.[7] Such calculations
would certainly diminish the estimated cosmological age.
Recent model research has bolstered this concept.

Joao Magueijo, a Royal Society research fellow at Imperial
College, London, and Andreas Albrecht, of the University
of California at Davis, say the speed of light immediately
after the universe was born may have been far faster than
its present value. . . . They say it has been slowing down
ever since. . . . The effects predicted by the theory are to
be published in the scientific journal, *Physical Review D*.
One mystery that it seems to be able to explain is why
the universe is so uniform—why opposite extremes of the
cosmos that are so far apart to have ever been in contact
with each other appear to obey the same rules of physics
and are at about the same temperature.[8]

Edward F. Blick (professor of aerodynamics, nuclear engineering, and geological engineering at the University of Oklahoma) refers to various reports that give **age of the moon rocks** brought back to earth by Apollo astronauts as ranging from two billion to eight billion years. He then shows that credible scholars have pointed out serious flaws in the dating method, and relates a recent age determination. "Scientists at Rice University and other well-known scientists such as Melvin Cook, Nobel Prize medalist, say that their analysis indicates the moon rocks are perhaps at the oldest, ten thousand years of age."[9]

The area of greatest interest in our current discussion is the **age of the earth.** The most familiar reference for age dating is that of radiocarbon. But modern technology has shown this method to be flawed as well.

> The troubles of the radiocarbon dating method are undeniably deep and serious. . . . [T]he underlying *assumptions* have been strongly challenged, and warnings are out that radiocarbon may soon find itself in a serious crisis situation. . . . No matter how "useful" it is . . . the radiocarbon method is still not capable of yielding accurate and reliable results. There are gross discrepancies, the chronology is uneven and relative, and the accepted dates are actually selected dates.[10]

The same is true with any radioactive substance used to give readings over extensive periods of time. Evolutionist William Stansfield made the point rather forcefully.

> It is obvious that radiometric techniques may not be the absolute dating methods that they are claimed to be. Age estimates on a given geological stratum by different radiometric methods are often quite different (sometimes

by hundreds of millions of years). There is no absolutely reliable long-term radiological "clock."[11]

Noted scholar Thomas Barnes, former dean of the ICR Graduate School and emeritus professor of physics at the University of Texas, El Paso, has demonstrated scientifically that the earth is young. His work deals with the decay of the earth's magnetic field.[12] The field has been measured as losing energy and intensity at an exponential rate. When projected back in time, the intensity of this field fifteen thousand years ago would have been so great that many of the molecules necessary for life could not have held together. With these considerations the outer limits of earth history falls within ten thousand years.[13] This work has been confirmed and extended by Sandia National Laboratory physicist D. Russell Humphreys.[14]

The science of population statistics also offers a major obstacle to ancient-earth models. According to evolutionary theory, Dawn Man and his mate appeared about two and a half million years ago. Experts have run calculations to determine whether this is possible. Over an extended period of time population growth has averaged less than two percent per year. However, about every eighty years one-third of the population is wiped out by wars, disease, and disasters. The population begins anew with two-thirds of the previous number and begins to increase at a little less than two percent per year. This average has held true for recorded history.

Young earth models include Noah's flood, where the population began anew with eight people less that forty-five hundred years ago. Using the science of population statistics, this would give us slightly over five billion people on the earth today.

Now we catch sight of the real problem. Using the same

conservative values, long-age evolution hits a brick wall. The population after only forty-one thousand years would be 2 x 10^{89}. Put simply, *there is not enough room to pack this number of bodies in the entire known universe!*[15]

Research scientist Robert Gentry has introduced a monumental work on radiohalos. His research has been published in numerous technical journals, and has not been successfully controverted. Gentry demonstrates that the granite (earth's foundation rock) was formed in a very short timespan, rather than the supposed 300 million–year timespan evolutionists postulate.[16]

In 1988 global attention was drawn to research termed "The Search for Adam and Eve."[17] In this article scientists claimed to have found our common ancestor—a woman who lived two hundred thousand years ago and left resilient genes that are carried by all of mankind. This research was centered around the mutation rate, or "clock," of mitochondrial DNA. Now current molecular research has determined that mtDNA appears to mutate much faster than expected, prompting new DNA forensics procedures and raising troubling questions about the dating of evolutionary events. In some controlled studies the mutation rate is twenty-fold faster. Using the new clock the woman who supposedly lived two hundred thousand years ago would be a mere six thousand years old![18]

Astrophysicist Russell Humphreys of Sandia National Laboratory lists (and documents) fifteen reasons why the earth and the universe cannot be old:

1. Galaxies wind themselves up too fast
2. Comets disintegrate too quickly
3. Earth's continents erode too fast
4. Not enough sediment on the sea floors
5. The ocean accumulates sodium too fast

6. The earth's magnetic field is decaying too fast
7. Multilayer fossils straddle too many strata
8. Many strata are too tightly bent
9. Out-of-sequence fossils scramble the timetable
10. Fossil radioactivity shortens "geologic ages" to a few years
11. Not enough helium in earth's atmosphere
12. Too much helium in hot rocks
13. Not enough stone age skeletons
14. Agriculture is too recent
15. Recorded history is too short[19]

In *The Illustrated Origins Answer Book*, Paul Taylor lists 102 scientific research projects that demonstrate young-earth calculations. Technical sources and citations are included.[20]

Perhaps the best way to close this section is to quote evolutionist Frederick Jueneman.

There has been in recent years the horrible realization that radio-decay rates are not as constant as previously thought, nor are they immune to environmental influences. And this could mean that the atomic clocks are reset during some global disaster, and events which brought the Mesozoic to a close may not be 65-million years ago, but rather, within the age and memory of man.[21]

Evolution won't work because of the sparse commodity called "time." And it also faces the problem of . . .

---

1. R. Cowen, "Further Evidence of a Youthful Universe," *Science News*, Vol. 148, September 9, 1995, p. 166
2. Harold S. Slusher, *The Origin of the Universe* (El Cajon, CA: Institute for Creation Research, 1980), p. 52
3. Hadley Wood, *Unveiling the Universe* (New York: American Elsevier

Publishing Company, 1968), p. 188

4. C. B. Clason, *Exploring the Distant Stars* (New York: G. P. Putnam's Sons, 1958), p. 326

5. T. Norman and B. Setterfield, *The Atomic Constants, Light, and Time* (Adelaide, Australia: Technical Monograph, Flinders University, 1987)

6. D. Russell Humphries, *Starlight and Time* (Green Forest, AR: Master Books, 1994)

7. Steve Farrar, "Speed of Light Slowing Down," *The London Sunday Times* (Britain, November 15, 1998)

8. M. A. Cook, "Rare Gas Absorption on Solids of the Lunar Regolith," *Journal of Colloid and Interface Science*, Vol. 38, No. 1, January 1972

9. Edward F. Blick, *A Scientific Analysis of Genesis* (Oklahoma City, OK: Hearthstone Publishing, 1991), p. 38

10. Robert E. Lee, "Radiocarbon, Ages in Error," *Anthropological Journal of Canada*, Vol. 19, No. 3, 1981, pp. 9,29

11. William D. Stansfield, *The Science of Evolution* (New York: Macmillan, 1977), p. 84

12. Thomas Barnes, *Origin and Destiny of Earth's Magnetic Field* (El Cajon, CA: ICR Technical Monograph #4, 1983)

13. Thomas Barnes, "Dwindling Resource Evidence of a Young Earth," *Creation Research Society Quarterly*, Vol. 25, No. 4 (Terre Haute, IN, March 1989), pp. 170–71

14. D. Russell Humphreys, "The Creation of the Earth's Magnetic Field," *Creation Research Society Quarterly*, Vol. 20, No. 2 (Terre Haute, IN, September 1983), p. 92

15. John D. Morris, *The Young Earth*, (Master Books, Green Forest, AR, 1997) p. 70

16. Robert V. Gentry, "Letters," *Physics Today*, Vol. 36, No. 4, April 1983, p. 13

17. Douglas Wallace, "The Search for Adam and Eve," Science Section, *Newsweek*, January 11, 1988, pp. 46–52

18. Ann Gibbons, "Calibrating the Mitochondrial Clock," *Science*, Vol. 279, January 2, 1998, pp. 28–29

19. D. Russell Humphrey, "Evidence for a Young World," *Answers in Genesis* (P. O. Box 6330, Florence, KY 41022)

20. Paul S. Taylor, *The Illustrated Origins Answer Book* (Mesa, Arizona: Films for Christ, 1989), pp. 18–20

21. Frederick B. Jueneman, "Secular Catastrophism," *Industrial Research and Development*, Vol. 24, June 1982, p. 21

Chapter 9

Design

Evolutionary scholars are forced to admit that "design" is found in the structure of our planet and throughout the known universe. Adept minds are recognizing the "Anthropic Principle," that is, that **the universe was designed for life.** To secularists, this is just a fortunate set of circumstances; to theistic evolutionists, this is a "window" of viability in the divinely monitored development of the universe from a "big bang"; to progressive creationists, this represents God's episodic intervention in the natural realm He initiated.

But nearly two centuries ago William Paley demonstrated in *Natural Theology* that the extreme sophistication of living systems (and their ecological support systems) required **a direct and original intelligent design in all its components—by a Master.**[1] Overshadowing all the decay and rebellion seen throughout nature, the biblical creationists sees **the direct hand of God in creation.** Man's benefit and the Creator's glory are seen as the ultimate purpose in this orchestrated symphony of design.

In the beginning God created the heaven and the earth.[2]

All things were made by him; and without him was not

any thing made that was made.[3]
For in six days the LORD made heaven and earth, the sea,
and all that in them is.[4]

He hath made the earth by his power, he hath established
the world by his wisdom, and hath stretched out the
heaven by his understanding.[5]

This direct design, requiring an all-encompassing Designer is observed from the macrocosm to the microcosm.
Here we outline the path of observation.

I. Universal Design . . .

Physicists have stumbled on signs that the cosmos is
custom-made for life and consciousness. It turns out that
if the constants of nature—unchanging numbers like the
strength of gravity, the charge of an electron, and the mass
of a proton—were the tiniest bit different, then atoms
would not hold together, stars would not burn, and life
would never have made an appearance. . . . It turns out
that the largest size imaginable, the entire universe, is
10 with 29 zeroes after it (in centimeters). The smallest
size describes the subatomic world, and it is 10 with 24
zeroes (and a decimal) in front of it. **Humans are right
in the middle. . . .** Our minds, which invent mathematics, conform to the reality of the cosmos. We are somehow
tuned to its truths. Since pure thought can penetrate
the universe's mysteries, this seems to be telling us that
something about human consciousness is harmonious
with the mind of God.[6]

II. Solar System Design . . .

Naturalistic explanations for the evolution of the solar
system . . . are unscientific and hopelessly inadequate. . . .

All planets should spin in the same direction, but Venus, Uranus, and Pluto rotate backward. All sixty-three moons in our solar system should orbit their planets in the same sense, but at least six have backward orbits. Furthermore, Jupiter, Saturn, and Neptune have moons orbiting in both directions. . . . The sun should have seven hundred times more angular momentum than all the planets combined. Instead, the planets have fifty times more angular momentum than the sun.[7]

Under close scrutiny evolutionary scenarios fail to explain the origin and function of the solar system. It was uniquely designed.

III. Planetary Design . . .
Earth is at a critical distance from the sun. If this distance had been only five percent closer, the atmosphere's greenhouse effect would have raised the surface temperature to nine hundred degrees Fahrenheit. An increase of the earth's distance from the sun by a mere one percent would evoke a period of uncontrolled or runaway glaciation.[8]

IV. Ecological Design . . .
Earth's remarkable hydrologic cycle has been cited as a display of fine-tuned design. (See Ecclesiastes 1:6–7 and Isaiah 55:10). Within this ecological habitat all systems are interrelated. Secular scholars cannot ignore symbiotic relationships. Of special note is the bee orchid and the orchid genus *Eucera,* as well as the fig wasp and the fig tree.[9] (See the video series *Creation in Sympathy: The Evidence.*)

A recent addition to the list includes a three-wattled bellbird that waggles and booms in a tropical fruit tree called *Ocotea endresiana.* The bellbird performs his romantic ceremony while dropping the tropical seeds in a clearing where the sun's rays can reach the future seedlings.[10]

V. Biologic Design . . .

. . . The elegance and complexity of biological sytems at the molecular level have paralyzed science's attempt to explain their origins. . . . There are compelling reasons— based on the structure of the systems themselves—to think that a Darwinian explanation for the mechanisms of life will forever prove elusive.[11]

If it could be demonstrated that any complex organ existed which could not possibly have been formed by numerous, successive, slight modifications, my theory would absolutely break down.[12]

To Darwin, the cell was a "black box"—its inner workings were utterly mysterious to him. Now, the black box has been opened up and we know how it works. Applying Darwin's test to the ultra-complex world of molecular machinery and cellular systems that have been discovered over the past forty years, we can say that Darwin's theory has "absolutely broken down."[13]

The "ultra-complex world of molecular machinery" can be illustrated by the incredible bacterial flagellum, an actual rotating bacterial motor! (see page 128).

The *neck of the giraffe* has been an object of marvel to those involved with design study.

. . . The giraffe is equipped with . . . a coordinated system of blood pressure control. Pressure sensors along the neck's arteries monitor the blood pressure, and can signal activation of other mechanisms to counter any increase in pressure as the giraffe drinks or grazes. Contraction of the artery walls, a shunting of part of the arterial blood flow to bypass the brain, and a web of small blood vessels (the *rete mirabile,* or marvelous net) between the arteries and the brain all serve to control the blood pressure in the giraffe's head.[14]

There is no conceivable naturalistic explanation for this marvel. Without all these items of the coordinated blood pressure system in place at the same time, the creature would have passed out from lack of oxygen when he elevated his head to full stature—or would have hemorrhaged from excessive blood pressure upon bowing his head to drink!

As the giraffe drinks, an adaptational package protects it from hemorrhaging in the brain:

Pressure sensors along the arteries detect rise in pressure

Heavily valved veins control return of blood to heart

Increased muscle fiber in the artery walls toward head allows greater control through artery constriction

Some arteries approaching the head branch into rete mirabile, others bypass brain

Rete mirabile

Brain

© 1999 by Steve Miller

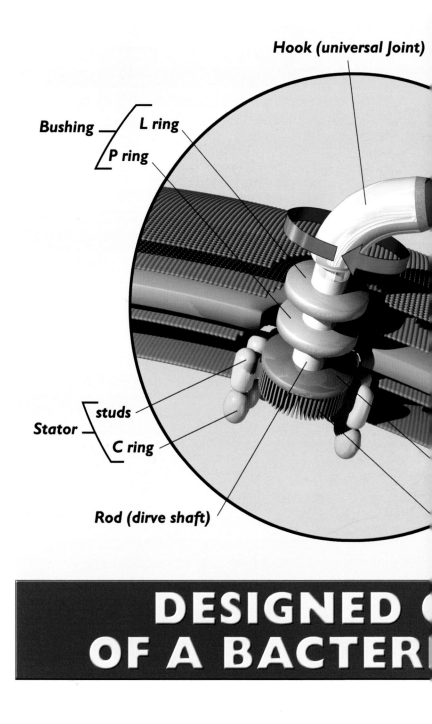

Hook (universal Joint)

Bushing — L ring
P ring

Stator — studs
C ring

Rod (dirve shaft)

DESIGNED (
OF A BACTER

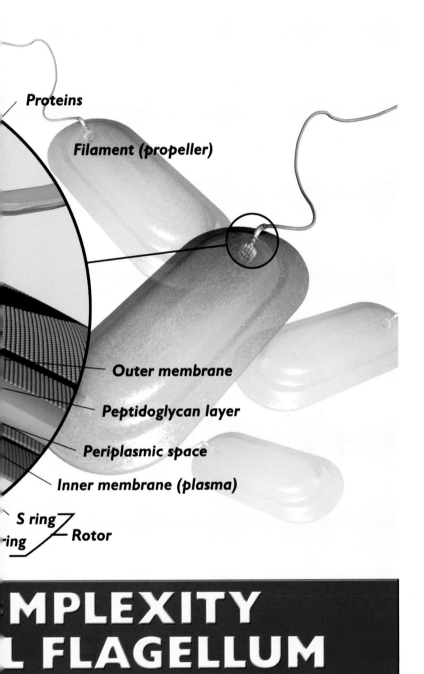

Proteins

Filament (propeller)

Outer membrane

Peptidoglycan layer

Periplasmic space

Inner membrane (plasma)

S ring

ring

Rotor

MPLEXITY

L FLAGELLUM

One hundred fifty years ago scientists were not qualified to explore the incredibly complex structures within cells, or even within biological organs. Yet, there was enough information to impress informed researchers as to the extreme improbability of evolving eyes. Charles Darwin knew then when he wrote:

> To suppose that the eye, with all its inimitable contrivances for adjusting the focus to different distances, for admitting different amounts of light, and for the correction of spherical and chromatic aberration, could have been formed by natural selection seems, I freely confess, absurd in the highest possible degree.[15]

Scientists are now aware of the fact that the eye is interrelated with respiratory and cardiovascular systems, as well as massive sections of the brain.[16]

A most interesting discourse on design within structural organs has been brought to light by professor M. E. Clark of the University of Illinois. As a recognized specialist in fluid mechanics and biomechanics, professor Clark points to the "Circle of Willis" in demonstrating optimal design within the human cardiovascular system. This marvelous arterial configuration is a feature of the blood supply providing ultimate safety for the delivery of oxygen to the brain (see page 132).[17]

Professor Clark continues his demonstration of optimal design by relating the incredible *pre-design* in the heart of the unborn child. A valve which originally was open during gestation closes automatically at the moment of birth, permitting optimal reception of enriched blood to the infant's brain.[18]

Additional pre-design is evidenced in the exchange of antibodies from the mother's milk to the receptive infant:

Breast milk comes equipped with antibodies that a woman generates and passes on to her infant. . . . One such antibody works against rotavirus, the most common cause of diarrhea in infants. Now, researchers in the United States and Mexico have discovered that a complex carbohydrate in breast milk affords babies even more protection than the antibody specifically made to fight the disease.[19]

VI. Human Brain Design
The human mind **is the ultimate and consummate expression of organ design.**

. . . I am fearfully and wonderfully made: marvelous are thy works; and that my soul knoweth right well.[20]

Who hath put wisdom in the inward parts? or who hath given understanding to the heart?[21]

I will put my laws into their mind, and write them in their hearts. . . .[22]

. . . Our brain's structure and function is unique to our species, and is the source of our humanness. The brain is therefore the ultimate key to that innermost sanctum of understanding, wherein we may find the secret of the human spirit.[23]

To appreciate the uniqueness of the human brain, modern science was required to invent new instruments and new terminology in an attempt to explain this awesome organ.

A. *Physical dimensions of the human mind. . .*
. . . The conscious brain wherein reside reason, judgment, and memory…plus all other parts of brain, occupy the

The Amazing "CIRCLE OF WILLIS"
in the Design of Brain Circulation

Located directly above the roof of the mouth is what is called *"The Circle of Willis."* The blood to the brain is here 'pooled,' divided, and then distributed by another system of arteries to the various lobes of the brain according to the particular requirements of the arterial beds. If a supply vessel is somehow occluded, the total supply is somewhat reduced; however, because of the parallel nature of the cerebral network, the blood that reaches the circle is distributed in the same proportion as that which occurred in the normal situation. The reason for this providential provision is that the flow distribution is determined mainly by the resistance distribution in the arterial beds. When a supply vessel is occluded, the resistance pattern in the terminal beds is not materially altered. Therefore, the blood is distributed in a somewhat reduced but normal pattern—each subsystem getting its fair share of whatever blood gets to the circle of Willis. What an amazing design by our Divine Designer!

Circle of Willis
Supplies blood to:

anterior cerebrum

anterior communication

middle cerebrum

internal carotid

posterior communication

posterior cerebrum

anterior cerebellum

posterior cerebellum

basilar

vertebrae

space of a quart container and weigh a total of about three pounds. Though the three pounds represent a mere two percent of the body weight . . . the quartful of brain is so metabolically active that it uses twenty percent of the oxygen we take in through our lungs. . . . Of the total

The *hemispheres* of the brain are subdivided into lobes, each of which is characterized by unique functional capacities. The planning of the future utilizes the *frontal lobes (A)*. Musical masters' concerti are heard and appreciated through the action of the *temporal lobes (B)*. The *occipital lobes (C)* of the hemispheres are responsible for the visual capacities necessary to construct the architectural monuments of the world. The logic of mathematics, representing perhaps the most abstract of neural functions, is derived in part from the *parietal lobes (D)*.

Circle of Willis

Circle of Willis

COMPLEXITY OF THE HUMAN BRAIN

The human brain consists of about ten thousand million nerve cells. Each nerve cell puts out somewhere in the region of between ten thousand and one hundred thousand connecting fibers by which it makes contact with other nerve cells in the brain. Altogether the total number of connections in the human brain approaches 10^{15} or a thousand million million. Numbers in the order of 10^{15} are of course completely beyond comprehension. Imagine an area about half the size of the USA (one million square miles) covered in a forest of trees containing ten thousand trees per square mile. If each tree contained one hundred thousand leaves, the total number of leaves in the forest would be 10^{15}, equivalent to the number of connections in the human brain!

of about 50,000 to 100,000 genes in Homo *sapiens*, some 30,000 code for one or another aspect of the brain.[24] ... The brain is different and immeasurably more complicated than anything else in the known universe.[25]

The physical brain is comprised of over 100 billion cells, each with over 50,000 neuron connections to other brain cells.[26] This structure receives over 100 million separate signals from the total human body every second. If we learned something new each second of our lives, it would take three million years to exhaust the capacity of the brain.[27]

B. Capabilities of the human mind . . .

The brain allows the finger to feel vibrations of 8/1000 of an inch. It allows the eye to see 10 million different colors.[28] The brain directs the:

1. Central Nervous System
2. Peripheral Nervous System
3. Autonomic Nervous System

. . . all in concert with the rest of the amazing human body!

The brain supports its own optimal blood flow with the designed mechanism called the "Circle of Willis" at its base.[29]

Phenomenal brain function is illustrated in the **idiot savant syndrome** (damage to the left hemisphere during fetal development results in greater development in the right hemisphere). While these individuals are mentally retarded, they are able to perform incredible mental feats:

Jedediah Buxton lived in the 1700s and, as an adult, had a mental age of ten. When asked how many 1/8-inch cubes existed in an area 23,145,789 yards by 5,642,732 yards by 54,965 yards, he gave the *correct 28-digit number,* then volunteered to give it backward.

"K" as an adult has a mental age of eleven and a working vocabulary of fifty-eight words. Yet, he can give you the name and population of every U.S. city over five thousand in population, every county seat in the nation, distances of every town from Chicago to New York, and a list of over two thousand hotels (with names, locations, and number of rooms).

Leslie Lemke is blind and mentally retarded, yet plays the piano masterfully. He can play any musical rendition *after one hearing*, and can play it flawlessly the rest of his life. This includes classical works especially. He once played every note of a *forty-five–minute orchestral rendition after a single exposure*.

C. The mind's influence on the rest of the human body . . .

"We do know that *thoughts* determine moods, and moods reflect changes in both hormonal ctivity and immune function."[30] "The body heals itself."[31] "The brain controls the immune system the same way it controls behavioral activities."[32] "Scientists discover the links between the brain and your health."[33]

D. The mind's response to the Creator . . .

"The uniquely human 'consciousness'—variously defined as language, introspection, self-awareness, and abstract thinking—*eludes scientific measurement* [emphasis added]."[34] "People can actually reason, anticipate consequences, and devise plans—all without knowing they are doing so."[35] *We respond because we were designed to respond!*

VII. Cellular Design . . .

. . . The cells have many different compartments in which different tasks are performed. . . . A cell has specialized areas partitioned off for discrete tasks. These areas include the *nucleus* (where the DNA resides), the *mitochondria* (which produces the cell's energy), the *endoplasmic reticulum* (which processes proteins), the *lysosome* (the cells garbage disposal unit), secretory *vesicles* (which store cargo before it must be sent out of the cell), and the *perosixome* (which helps metabolize fats). Each com-

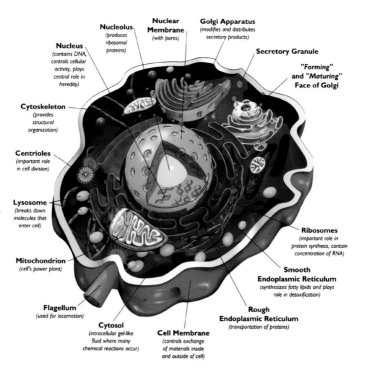

partment is sealed off from the rest of the cell by its own membrane. . . . The *membranes* themselves can also be considered separate compartments, because the cell places material into membranes that is not found elsewhere. . . . There are more than **twenty different sections in a cell.** . . . A single flaw in the cell's labyrinthine protein-transport pathway is fatal. Unless the entire system were immediately in place, our ancestors would have suffered a similar fate. Attempts at a gradual evolution of the protein transport system are a recipe for extinction.[36]

A typical cell contains about ten million million atoms.[37] Biochemists assert that all systems of the cell must be in place—and functioning —for the cell to operate at all. Their interrelated and interdependent components are illustrated.

VIII. Genetic Design ...

Henry Morris, founder of the Institute for Creation Research, comments on this issue, referring to Psalm 139:15:

" C u riously wrought" means "embroidered," a striking description of the double-helical

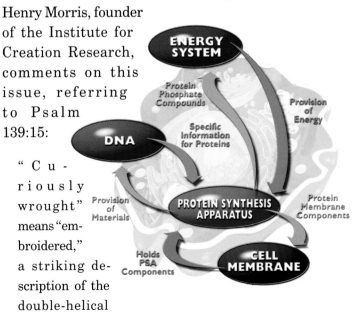

ENERGY SYSTEM

Protein Phosphate Compounds

Provision of Energy

DNA

Specific Information for Proteins

Provision of Materials

PROTEIN SYNTHESIS APPARATUS

Protein Membrane Components

Holds PSA Components

CELL MEMBRANE

> DNA *molecular program* which organizes part by part
> the beautiful structure of the whole infant. . . . He [God]
> created within the body of Adam and Eve the marvelous
> and complex ability to multiply that body and to generate
> from these lowest parts of the earth through the curiously
> wrought embroidery of DNA, all the many billions of their
> descendants including David himself.[38]

The tremendous body of information comprising the human genome is contained in just three percent of the DNA structure. The remaining ninety-seven percent has been referred to as "junk DNA." But evidence is now becoming available to indicate that this is not "junk," but instead is organized for some distinct purpose.

The protein-coding portion of the genes account for only about three percent of the DNA in the human genome; the other ninety-seven percent encodes no proteins. Most of this enormous, silent genetic majority has long been thought to have no real function—hence its name: "junk DNA." But one researcher's trash is another researcher's treasure, and a growing number of scientists believe that hidden in the junk DNA are intellectual riches.[39]

Eugene Stanley of Boston University found evidence that much of the nonprotein-coding DNA has informational characteristics resembling those of a human language.[40]

IX. Atomic Design . . .

Representatives of every class of *atoms* in the periodic

table are necessary for life. . . . Each atom consists of a nucleus . . . and a series of seven concentric electron orbits.[41]

The fact that the living systems require *exactly* what has been provided points to the nurturing care of an all-wise Designer. The incidence of "sevens" throughout inorganic and organic systems displays purposeful arrangement throughout the creation.

X. Subatomic Design . . .

Physicists recognize four fundamental forces. These largely determine the way in which *one bit of matter or radiation* can interact with another.[42]

The numerical values that nature has assigned to the fundamental constants such as the charge of the electron, the mass of the proton, and the Newtonian gravitational constant, may be mysterious, but they are critically relevant to the structure of the universe that we perceive. . . . Had nature opted for a slightly different set of numbers, the world would be a very different place. Probably we would not be here to see it.[43]

This author is convinced that it was more than "nature" which opted for optimal and exhaustive universal arrangement, but was, instead, the concerted action of a personal, supernatural Creator.

1. William Paley, *Natural Theology,* American Tract Society, New York, pp. 9–10
2. Genesis 1:1
3. John 1:3
4. Exodus 20:11
5. Jeremiah 51:15
6. Sharon Begley, quoting John Polkinghorne, Joel Primack, and Carl

Feit, "Science Finds God," *Newsweek,* July 20, 1998, pp. 46–51

7. Walt Brown, "Astronomical and Physical Sciences," *In the Beginning* (Phoenix, AZ: Center for Scientific Creation, 1997), p. 17

8. Ron Cattrell, *The Remarkable Spaceship Earth* (Denver: Accent Books, 1982), pp. 44–45

9. Macmillan, *The Way Nature Works* (New York: Macmillan Company, 1992), pp. 125, 136–7, 192–3, 195, 198

10. S. Milius, "Romantic display gets tree planted," *Science News,* Vol. 153, May 30, 1998

11. Michael J. Behe, *Darwin's Black Box* (New York: The Free Press, 1996), p. X

12. Charles Darwin, quoted in "Meeting Darwin's Wager," *Christianity Today,* April 28, 1997, p. 15

13. Michael J. Behe, quoted in *Christianity Today,* ibid.

14. Percival Davis, Dean H. Kenyon, and Charles B. Thaxton, *Of Pandas and People* (Dallas: Haughton Publishing Company, 1989), p. 71

15. Charles Darwin, *The Origin of Species by Natural Selection,* first edition reprint (New York: Avenel Books, 1979), p. 217 (Chapter 6, "Difficulties in Theory"); first edition: 1859.

16. Mark Eastman, M.D., "From Goo to the Zoo to You," *Creation vs. Evolution,* Chuck Missler audio series, 1998

17. M. E. Clark, *Paley Watches in the Blood Stream,* 2020 Zuppke, Champaign-Urbana, IL 61801

18. M. E. Clark, "Optimal Design in Cardiovascular Fluid Mechanics," *Personal Monograph*

19. *Science News,* Vol. 153, May 16, 1998, p. 317

20. Psalm 139:14

21. Job 38:36

22. Hebrews 8:10

23. Sherwin B. Nuland, *The Wisdom of the Body* (New York: Alfred A. Knopf, 1997) p. 327

24. Ibid., p. 328

25. Richard M. Restak, *The Brain: The Last Frontier,* 1979, p. 390

26. *The Brain, Our Universe Within,* PBS Video

27. *Wonders of God's Creation,* Moody Video Series

28. Paul A. Bartz, *Letting God Create Your Day* (Minneapolis: Bible Science Association, 1993), Vol. 4, p. 197

29. M. E. Clark, "Safety Mechanism for the Cerebral Circulation," *Paley Watches in the Blood Stream*

30. David S. Sobel, M.D. and Robert Ornstein, Ph.D., *The Healthy Mind Healthy Body,* (New York: Time Life Medical, 1996), p. 41

31. Sherry Baker, "Internal Medicine," *Omni,* January 1991, p. 77

32. Rob Wechsler, "A New Prescription: Mind Over Malady," *Discover,* February 1987, p. 50

33. *Newsweek,* November 1988, p. 88

34. Joel L. Swerdlow, "Miracles of the Brain," *National Geographic*, June 1995, p. 133
35. Joseph Weiss, "Unconscious Mental Functioning," *Scientific American*, March 1990, p. 103
36. Behe, ibid., pp. 103, 114
37. Michael Denton, *Evolution: A Theory in Crisis* (London: Burnett Books, Ltd., 1985), p. 329
38. Henry M. Morris, *The Defender's Study Bible* (Grand Rapids: Word Publishing, 1995), p. 669
39. Rachel Nowak, "Mining Treasures from 'Junk DNA,'" *Science,* Vol. 263, February 4, 1994, p. 608
40. Editorial, "Hints of a Language in Junk DNA," *Science*, November 25, 1994
41. Michael J. Denton, *Nature's Destiny* (New York: The Free Press, 1998), pp. 71, 74
42. Ibid., p. 12
43. P. C. W. Davies, *The Accidental Universe* (Cambridge: Cambridge University Press, 1982), preface

Chapter 10

Why Good Men Believe Bad Science

Serious students of the creation/evolution controversy would readily admit that the foregoing references are by no means exaggerated or taken out of context. But mainstream academia has adopted evolution as if it were fact set in stone. Henry Morris and John Morris list areas in which evolutionary explanations play a dominant role:

1. Anthropology
2. Biology
3. Cosmology
4. Ecology
5. Education
6. Ethics
7. Exobiology
8. Geology
9. Philosophy
10. Population growth
11. Psychology
12. Religion
13. Social sciences[1]

Often the interpretation and publication of data depend more on the "mindset" of the researcher or instructor than the facts warrant. Data can be manipulated to support favored notions. Theodosius Dobzhansky asserted that "evolution is a light which illuminates all facts, a trajectory which all lines of thought must follow."[2]

This realization that a "mindset" can, knowingly or unknowingly, justify an unwarranted conclusion is not an original observation. In a review of Richard Leakey's book, *Origins: What New Discoveries Reveal About the Emergence of Our Species and Its Possible Future*, Yale professor of anthropology David Pilbeam made some rather sobering comments about the fossil evidence for man's origin as seen from an evolutionary viewpoint:

> My reservations concern not so much this book but the whole subject and methodology of paleoanthropology.... Perhaps generations of students of human evolution, including myself, have been flailing about in the dark; that our data base is too sparse, too slippery, for it to be able to mold our theories. **Rather the theories are more statements** about **us and ideology than about the past. Paleoanthropology reveals more about how humans view themselves than it does about how humans came about** [emphasis added].[3]

Since "paleoanthropology reveals more about how humans view themselves than it does about how humans came about," we need to examine **why** many scholars justify their evolutionary approach—and in essence **rule out the supernatural** while **deifying the natural**.

On the surface this adoption of evolutionary persuasions appears to be the result of one or more of the following:

1. Misinformation about *evidence* "for" or "against" evolution

2. Desire to appear *"intellectual"* to self or peers
3. Influence by *associates or instructors*
4. *Reaction* to "restrictive" individuals
5. *Preference* toward the erotic
6. Escape from *accountability* to a deity

But the surface persuasions fall on fertile ground. The "soil of the soul" is prepared by the individual's response to real life situations. Writing in *Scientific American,* psychotherapist Joseph Weiss reports on unconscious mental functioning and the mind's ability to make strategic decisions, often without the person being consciously aware that he is doing so. He reveals that "people can actually reason, anticipate consequences and devise plans—all without knowing they are doing so. Patients apply such skills in the service of getting well [or preferring to remain ill, or adopting a mindset]."[4]

Professor Gunther S. Stent (instructor in molecular biology at the University of California at Berkeley) refers to "an 'inner man' who transforms visual image into a precept."[5] (The reader will recall the "morphing" illustration in chapter two.)

This "inner man who transforms visual images into a precept" is exposed to an added dimension. Current research in neuroscience indicates that, while the human mind has been slow to give up its secrets, specific areas of the physical brain respond with distinctive experiences that are the result of genetic programming in the very makeup of man. Within the limbic system of the brain (an actual physical component of its structure) is designed a capacity which has astounded modern scientific researchers. When this area is gently stimulated with electromagnetic energy during clinical laboratory procedures, **the patient senses the presence of God!**[6, 7]

The limbic system gets its input from all sensory systems—vision, touch, hearing, taste and smell. . . . [This system] constitutes a central core processing system of the brain that deals with information derived from events, memories of events and emotional associations of these events.[8]

It seems very unlikely that any creature other than humans can ponder the infinite or wonder about "the meaning of it all."[9]

Uniquely, our sensory images and the precepts we embrace are actually formulated in a context involving a subliminal awareness of God's presence.

Realizing this incredible and unique capacity of the human mind, we are better prepared to understand why many individuals "self-determine" a commitment to evolutionary theory, often against known evidence and against all odds. **The individual's personal response to real life situations involving his interpretation of divine involvement** determines the degree of *personal tranquillity* or *"inner anguish"* held by that individual. And, intense self-imposed "inner anguish" foments resentment toward whoever (or Whoever) is viewed as being responsible for the conditions in question. Charles Darwin "tapped" into a universal human experience.

If the total truth were known, there is a **universal human experience, common to all men,** that (in varying degrees) responds to suffering or loss with *phobic resentment.* The biblical record indicates that men first began to "deride" the name of the Lord when a "feable" child was born (Gen. 4:26). This is demonstrated to be the case with Darwin. Medical researchers have recently re-diagnosed his ills and reviewed his conditions as a whole to make *an overwhelming case for phobic panic disorder*.[10] Moreover, his experience with extreme phobias appears to be self-incubated.

> Darwin returned to England at twenty-seven in a robust state of mind and body. It was not until a year later, when he began to write in his evolutionary notebooks, that he first felt and commented on his illness, forcing himself into a lifetime of severe, repugnant, and sometimes ludicrous disability.[11]

His biographers describe him as a "tormented evolutionist." They report that he uttered, "It is like confessing to a murder," upon revealing what he "knew" to be true: that humans are descended from headless hermaphrodite squids.[12] Further investigation indicates that his admission to "murder" had as much to do with a dethronement of God as it did with a removal of man from any noble heritage.[13] He wrote in his autobiography:

> During these two years (October 1836 to January 1839) I was led to think much about religion. . . . But I had gradually come, by this time, to see that the Old Testament from its manifestly false history of the world, with the Tower of Babel, the rainbow as a sign, etc., and from its attributing to God the feelings of a revengeful tyrant, was no more to be trusted than the sacred books of the Hindus, or the beliefs of any barbarian. . . .
>
> Thus disbelief crept over me at a very slow rate, but was at last complete. . . . Although I did not think much about the existence of a personal God until a considerably later period in my life . . . the old argument of design in nature, as given by Paley, which formerly seemed to me

so conclusive, fails, now that the law of natural selection has been discovered. . . .

It would be as difficult for them to throw off their belief in God, as for a monkey to throw off its instinctive fear and hatred of a snake.[14]

Biologist Theodosius Dobzhansky vocalized what he and his colleagues knew mentor Charles Darwin had been saying all along—that which the general public was only now prepared to hear: "In giving rise to man, the evolutionary process has, apparently for the first and only time in the history of the Cosmos, become conscious of itself."[15]

Evolutionary socialist Jeremy Rifkin further expressed the sentiments:

Evolution is no longer viewed as a mindless affair, quite the opposite. It is mind enlarging its domain up the chain of species. . . . [O]ne eventually ends up with the idea of the universe as a mind that oversees, orchestrates, and gives order and structure to all things.[16]

Evolution endows matter with the ability to create its own existence[17] as it

- Inherits an infinite capacity to foresee future requirements[18] (omniscience)
- Enlists its own efforts to produce and sustain life[19] (omnipotence), and
- Incubates communication with all entities under its universal influence[20] (omnipresence).

Charles Darwin was the first person to ascribe deity to natural selection in the cosmos. He wrote:

It may metaphorically be said that natural selection is daily and hourly scrutinizing, throughout the world, the slightest variations [*omniscience*]; rejecting those that are bad, preserving and adding up all that are good [*omnipresence*]; silently and insensibly working, whenever and wherever opportunity offers, at the improvement of each organic being in relation to its organic and inorganic conditions of life [*omnipotence*] (brackets added).[21]

In time this cosmic expression manifests itself as man and realizes its own existence. In short, matter is God. This idea is consistent with the writings of Darwin who saw the universe as chaotic, yet progressive.[22] He wrote: "When thus reflecting I feel compelled to look to a First Cause having an intelligent mind to some degree analogous to that of man; and I deserve to be called a Theist."[23]

This patriarchal monarch of evolutionary thought saw the universe as progressing by chaotic means, and ultimately becoming conscious of its own existence *in his tormented mind.* He embodied the concept of insecure man in harmony with a discordant universe. In placing man as the ultimate product of a self-realizing universe, he replaced God with himself. *He thus worshipped himself!* Prophetic scriptures envision a time in the future when man will actually sit on a throne demanding universal worship.[24]

Darwin is elevated to the position of patriarchal monarch by a *kindred inner experience of turmoil* on the part of his devotees. Strangely, this inner turmoil is coupled with an inclination to self-admiration, which in turn produces a sense of inconsistency. This *kindred inner experience* may rest in hidden incipient stages, or it may reside in full-bloom phobic resentment. Following is a cyclical series of emotional steps that are often taken within a person's mind **in response to** *suffering* **or** *loss:*

1. Resentment toward persons viewed as responsible
2. Distrust of God
3. Appointment of self as Controller
4. Disturbing sense of chaos
5. Overwhelming fear
6. Entrenching phobias (expressed or subdued)

Steps one through three are exercised by choice within the mind of an individual. These are followed by steps four through six overtaking the emotions. Then the process starts all over again by reverting back to step one (resentment toward persons [or Person] thought to be responsible), with the experience deepening through each repetition. Adoption of chaos philosophy is then consistent with the inner turmoil experienced by the individual. Not all phobics become evolutionists, but it is a universal experience for an evolutionist to harbor reservations about a beneficent Creator, even if he is not conscious of such inner resentment.

This understanding gives us insight regarding the nature of evolutionary commitment. It is rarely a "commitment to truth." Rather, it is more often a move of desperation to incubate converts into sharing its "spirit of desperation." In fact, when the natural universe, its episodic events, and our personal experiences are viewed with a commitment to chaos theory, there is little evidence for hope. Chuck Missler aptly points out that, when "design" is eliminated from the equation,

- The law of entropy says, "You can't win."
- The law of mass action says, "You can't break even."
- The law of energy conservation says, "You can't even get out of the game!"[25]

The core of Darwin's theories has been discredited, yet he remains the patriarchal monarch of evolutionary theory. To repeat: this is due, primarily (and often unconsciously), to a "budding" **common experience of *internal resentment* on the part of each new convert.** If Charles Darwin had not come up with some modern "believable" mechanism to explain the introduction of human life by

Darwin Arguing With Himself

"less than divine" means, someone else would have! In fact, Alfred Russel Wallace independently set forth the same ideas as Darwin. Their papers on natural selection were actually read in public at the same time.[26] Why, then, is Wallace not credited with the same patriarchal status among evolutionists? Simply because he did not embody the same internal turmoil and resentment toward a personal God.

One of Darwin's primary tenets held that there could be no "ultimate answer" to basic issues. He relished being "bewildered."[27] Inconsistency was a part of the fabric in his theories. Likewise, humanism holds that *two mutually exclusive positions can be true*, so asserting that there can be no ultimate answers.[28]

Remember the four great questions of life? (Who am I? Where did I come from? What am I doing here? and, Where am I going?) If naturalistic evolution is embraced as a life-view, it leads inevitably to self as viewed with *a questionable identity, an uncertain past, a meaningless present, and a hopeless future*. This "less-than-special" appraisal of man is rather pervasive within the evolutionary community.

But there are signs of an encouraging stir, or at least a more candid admission in some areas. This candid appraisal begins by assessing the virtual impossibility of developing life from nonliving compounds. Consider the statement made by A. G. Cairns-Smith regarding the enormous gap between inorganic (nonliving) components and organic (living) systems:

[F]ar from there being a million ways in detail in which evolution could have got under way, there seems now to have been no obvious way at all. The singular feature is in the gap between the simplest conceivable version of organisms as we know them, and components that the Earth might reasonably have been able to generate. This gap can be seen more clearly now. *It is enormous* [emphasis added]. [29]

Scientists who utterly reject Evolution may be one of our fastest-growing controversial minorities. . . . Many of the scientists supporting this position hold impressive credentials in science.[30]

Astrophysicists Frederick Hoyle and Chandra Wichramasinghe wrote that some are even awakening to the realization that a Creator was involved in the scheme of things: "A super Intellect has monkeyed with the physics, as well as with chemistry and biology [of the universe]."[31]

Organic chemist Jay Roth of the University of Connecticut wrote along the same lines:

There is so much in the physical nature of the universe we inhabit, the exact balances of everything needed to support life, the piling of coincidence on coincidence, every one of which is vitally necessary for development of a stable star with a planet that can support life. These physical properties of the universe lead me to favor a Designer or Creator.[32]

Creation offers a plausible scientific model. Even non-traditional secular thinkers, like Frank Tipler, have come to a conclusion drawn from physics that

. . . the central claims of Judeo-Christian theology are in fact true, that these claims are straightforward deductions of the laws of physics as we now understand them. I have been forced into these conclusions by the inexorable logic of my special branch of physics.[33]

Tipler ultimately presents a concept of a non-personal God, a concept with which we certainly could not agree. However, he does embrace a scientific, physical analysis

> ... which is a testable physical theory for an omnipresent, omniscient, omnipotent God who will one day in the far future resurrect every single one of us to live forever in an abode which is in all essentials the Judeo-Christian Heaven. . . . I shall make no appeal, anywhere, to revelation. I shall appeal instead to the solid results of modern physical science.[34]

While his ultimate spiritual conclusions are unacceptable to this writer, Tipler nevertheless posits the material expression of the God of the Bible in the physical universe. In *Bioscience,* a leading biologist wrote about basic premises of science. He discussed such things as the principle of cause and effect, the unified nature of the world, etc. He then admitted that ". . . each of these postulates had its origin in, or was consistent with, Christian theology."[35]

While "science" as a whole has not embraced biblical appreciation, modern science has, nonetheless, been shown to be a direct outgrowth of the biblical worldview. In *Nature* this contention has been supported by Colin Russell:

> It is widely accepted on all sides that, far from undermining it, science is deeply indebted to Christianity and has been so from at least the scientific revolution. Recent historical research has uncovered many unexpected links between scientific enterprise and biblical theology.[36]

A remarkable thesis was written in *Encyclopaedia Britannica* demonstrating the unique contribution made by Christianity regarding our understanding of the universe:

> Augustine held that the universe is a created realm, brought into existence by God out of nothing (*ex nihilo*). It has no independent power of being, . . . but is through and through contingent, absolutely dependent upon the creative divine power. . . . This understanding of creation, entailing the universe's total emptiness of independent self-existence and yet its ultimate goodness as the free expression of God's creative love, is perhaps the most distinctively Christian contribution to metaphysical thought. . . . This basic Christian idea entails the value of creaturely life and of the material world itself, its dependence upon God, and the meaningfulness of the whole temporal process as fulfilling an ultimate divine purpose.[37]

In summary, evolution embodies the *frustrations* of:

1. *Questionable identity*
2. *Uncertain past*
3. *Meaningless present*
4. *Hopeless future*

Creation recognizes the worth of the individual whose *endowments* include:

1. *Identity with great value*
2. *Origin with created design*
3. *Existence with meaningful purpose*
4. *Future with unlimited hope.*

This researcher has great sympathy for those individuals held in the grips of an evolutionary mindset. I offer no harsh condemnation, but sincere sympathy and understanding. I have been there. There was a prolonged intellectual experience in my life that very privately embraced the tenets of evolution. I have felt the inner turmoil and the hopelessness of its consequences. The journey in the adoption of intellectual evolution is a journey of anguish. In pointing out the shortfalls of the theory, it is intended that the reader will be exposed to a better way—an avenue of hope, assurance, and truth.

Evolution requires an original miracle of stupendous proportions, suspends the laws of science (including cause and effect, conservation of mass and energy, entropy, biogenesis, DNA self-repair, lethal mutation damage), and invokes *a continuous succession of miracles against all scientific observations.*

The tenets of evolution are insisted upon AGAINST OVERWHELMING AND IMPOSSIBLE ODDS, and its justification exists only in the minds of its adherents.

In contrast, **special creation** recognizes the scientific principle of cause and effect, explores the handiwork of the Creator, and acknowledges that "of Him," "through Him," and "to Him" are all things.

To Him be glory forever.[38]

1. Henry M. Morris and John D. Morris, "Society & Creation," *The Modern Creation Trilogy*, (Green Forest, AR: Master Books 1996), p. 197
2. Francisco J. Ayala, "Nothing in Biology Makes Sense Except in the Light of Evolution, Theodosius Dobzhansky: 1900–1975," *Journal of Heredity*, Vol. 68, January/February 1997, pp. 3–10
3. David Pilbeam, review of *Origins*, by Richard E. Leakey and Roger Lewin (Dutton, 1977, 264 pp.), *American Scientist*, Vol. 66, May/June 1978, pp. 378–79
4. Joseph Weiss, "Unconscious Mental Functioning," *Scientific American*, Vol. 262, No. 3, March 1990, p. 103
5. Gunther S. Stent, "Limits to the Scientific Understanding of Man,"

Science, Vol. 187, March 21, 1975, p. 1054

6. Rita Carter, "A World of One's Own," *Mapping the Mind* (Berkeley, CA: University of California Press, 1998), p. 129

7. V. S. Ramachandran and Sandra Blakeslee, "God and the Limbic System," *Phantoms in the Brain* (New York: William Morrow & Company, 1998), pp. 175–98

8. Ibid., pp. 177–8

9. Ibid., p. 176

10. Thomas Barloon and Russel Noyes, "On the Origin of Darwin's Ills," *Discover*, September 1997, p. 27

11. Irving Stone, "The Death of Darwin," chapter 22 in *Darwin Up to Date*, ed. Jeremy Cherfas, (London: *New Scientist Guide*, IPC Magazines, Ltd., 1982), p. 69

12. Adrian Desmond and James Moore, *DARWIN, the Life of a Tormented Evolutionist* (New York: Time Warner Books, 1992), cover flap and p. 313f

13. Charles Darwin, "Autobiography," reprinted in *The Voyage of Charles Darwin*, edited by Christopher Rawlings (BBC, 1978), "A Scientist's Thoughts on Religion," *New Scientist*, Vol. 104, December 20/27, 1984, p. 75

14. Charles Darwin, *The Autobiography of Charles Darwin* (New York: Harcourt, Brace and Company, 1882), pp. 85,87,93

15. Theodosious Dobzhansky, "Changing Man," *Science*, Vol. 155, January 27, 1967, p. 409

16. Jeremy Rifkin, *Algeny* (New York: Viking Press, 1983), pp. 188,195

17. Li-Xin and J. Richard Gott III, op. cit.

18. Patrick Thaddeus, Mayo Greenberg, and Ben Clark, "The Road to Life," *Discover*, March 1998, pp. 69–72

19. Michael J. Denton, *Nature's Destiny* (New York: The Free Press, 1998), p. 269. He also quotes Robert Chambers, *Vestiges of the Natural History of Creation*, 1840

20. George M. Hall, "Blueprint of Evolution," *The Ingenious Mind of Nature* (New York: Plenum Trade, 1997), p. 273

21. Charles Darwin, 1872, *The Origin of Species,* pp. 82–84.

22. Charles Darwin, op. cit., p. 249

23. Ibid., p. 92

24. Second Thessalonians 2:3–4; Revelation 13:8

25. Chuck Missler, "The Creator Beyond Space and Time," *Creation vs. Evolution* audio series

26. Loren C. Eiseley, "Alfred Russel Wallace," *Scientific American*, Vol. 200, February 1959, p. 70

27. Charles Darwin, op. cit., p. 249

28. Humanist Manifesto II, *The Humanist*, September–October, 1973, Vol. XXXIII, No. 5

29. A. G. Cairn-Smith, *Seven Clues to the Origin of Life*: *A Scientific*

Detective Story, Cambridge University Press, 1985, p. 4

30. Larry Hatfield, "Educators Against Darwin," *Science Digest Special*, Winter 1979, pp. 94–96

31. Fred Hoyle and Chandra Wickramasinghe, *Evolution from Space*, (London: J. M. Dent and Company, 1981) pp. 141,144

32. Jay Roth quoted, authors: Henry Margenau and Roy Abraham Varghese, *Cosmos, Bios, Theos*, (La Salle, Illinois: Open Court, 1992) p. 197

33. Frank J. Tipler, *The Physics of Immortality*, (New York: Doubleday, 1994) p. ix

34. Ibid., p. 1

35. Stanley D. Beck, *Bioscience*, vol. 32, October 1982, p. 738

36. Colin Russell, *Nature*, vol. 308, April 26, 1984, p. 777

37. *Encyclopedia Britannica*, (Chicago: University of Chicago, 1990) Macropedia, vol. 16, p. 324

38. Romans 11:36

About the Author

Dr. Carl Edward Baugh is founder and director of Creation Evidence Museum, Glen Rose, Texas; scientific research director for world's first hyperbaric biosphere; scientific research director for water reclamation and energized plant systems; and the discoverer and excavation director of two major dinosaurs: *Acrocanthosaurus* in Texas and *Stegosaurus stenops* in Colorado.

He holds a Doctor of Theology degree from Louisiana Baptist University, a Masters in Archaeology, and a Doctor of Philosophy in Education from Pacific College of Graduate Studies.

He has appeared on the CBS TV network specials, "The Incredible Discovery of Noah's Ark" and "Ancient Secrets in the Bible"; on the NBC TV network special, "Mysterious Origins of Man"; and appeared on two national Japanese TV networks concerning dinosaurs and man; as well as conducted extensive interviews on ABC and CBS radio networks on Glen Rose excavations.

Dr. Baugh has been invited as a guest lecturer at NASA headquarters in Green Belt, Maryland, as a result of his independent research on the world's first hyperbaric biosphere. This biosphere is a simulation of the original ecospheric conditions of Planet Earth. Preliminary results show extended life spans (and enhanced size) of fruit flies, enhanced growth in fish, and structural alteration of snake venom. In his pioneering role as independent researcher in this field, he is president and CEO of Creation Research Systems, Inc.

More than thirty years of his life have been spent researching the atmospheric conditions before the Genesis flood. He has excavated an Indian princess for the archaeology department of the University of Texas. His recorded broadcasts include the only radio broadcast made atop Cheops Pyramid in Egypt.

Dr. Baugh is co-director of a research team (along with Dr.

Don Shockey) searching for Noah's Ark on Mt. Ararat in Turkey. He personally negotiated a forty-nine–year lease of Mt. Ararat with the Turkish government during the administration of President Uzal.

He has led three scientific expeditions into the rain forests of Papua New Guinea in search of living pterodactyls.

He is the founding director of the Creation Evidence Museum and oversees the hyperbaric biosphere's physical facility. His independent research involves the application of technology he has pioneered in biospheric science. This independent research includes hyperbaric pharmaceutical potentials in living plants and animals, energized water systems, energized systems for enhanced production of plants as food sources, energized systems for enhanced production of fishes, energized systems for enhanced production of livestock, and energized water recovery systems. Dr. Baugh's accredited doctoral degree and his doctoral dissertation are available on the Internet at: *www. creationevidence.org* or *www.creationism.org/cem/*.